Heinemann **Shakespeare** **New Edition**

The Merchant of Venice

SERIES EDITOR:
JOHN SEELY

EDITORIAL MATERIAL AND ACTIVITIES:
ELIZABETH SEELY
STUART McKEOWN
JOHN SEELY

Part of Pearson

Heinemann is an imprint of Pearson Education Limited, a company incorporated in England and Wales, having its registered office at Edinburgh Gate, Harlow, Essex, CM20 2JE. Registered company number: 872828

www.pearsonschoolsandfecolleges.co.uk

Heinemann is a registered trademark of Pearson Education Limited

First published 1994
This new edition published 2010

12 11 10
10 9 8 7 6 5 4 3 2 1

British Library Cataloguing in Publication Data
A catalogue record for this book is available from the British Library

ISBN 9780435026455

Typeset by Redmoor Design, Tavistock, Devon
Original illustrations © Pearson Education Limited, 2005
Illustrated by Roger Wade Walker
Cover photo © Photostage Ltd
Printed and bound in China (CTPS/01)

CONTENTS

The story of the play

Act 1

Scene 1

Antonio, a rich merchant in Venice, is depressed. He doesn't know why. His friends Salerio and Solanio suggest that he is concerned about the safety of his ships. He assures them that this is not a worry. Then they suggest he is in love. He denies this too. He has a close friend, Bassanio, who has many debts and owes a lot of money to Antonio. He has come now to explain that he needs more money to woo a rich and beautiful heiress, Portia, who lives in Belmont. Antonio hasn't any ready money, but he tells Bassanio to use his name to raise a loan.

Scene 2

Portia and her gentlewoman Nerissa are considering the method by which she must choose a husband. When her father died he was concerned that men would only want to marry her for her money. In the hope of avoiding this, he had three caskets prepared. One was of gold, the second of silver and the third of lead. The hopeful suitor must choose the correct one. The two women discuss the various suitors who have tried their luck. Each one who fails must promise never to marry. Portia disliked the first six, who left without trying. She is glad to see the back of them.

Scene 3

Bassanio has approached Shylock, a wealthy Jew, for the loan on Antonio's surety. Shylock knows that Antonio's riches depend on trade; he has several ships at sea at present and anything can happen to them. What really makes Shylock hate Antonio is the fact that he will lend money without charging interest. Interest on the money he lends is how Shylock makes his living. Shylock agrees to lend the money. But he suggests that if the money cannot be repaid by the due date, he will claim a pound of flesh from Antonio. Bassanio hates this idea but Antonio agrees.

Act 2

Scene 1

The Prince of Morocco has come to Belmont to try his luck. He has a high opinion of himself and his chances, but he must choose the right casket.

Scene 2

Launcelot, who is Shylock's servant, is trying to decide whether to leave his job or not, and he has an argument with his conscience. He meets his old father and sets out to confuse him. Then he asks Bassanio to take him on as a servant. Bassanio agrees. Bassanio's current servant is Leonardo and Bassanio orders him to make everything ready on the ship he will travel on to Belmont. His friend Gratiano begs to go with him and is allowed to do so.

Scene 3

Shylock's daughter, Jessica, is sorry that Launcelot is to leave. She hands him a letter for Lorenzo. They are in love.

Scene 4

Three of Antonio's friends and Lorenzo are planning their evening's entertainment. They are going to a masque. Lorenzo sends a message back to Jessica. She will steal money and jewels from her father for their elopement. This evening she will be Lorenzo's torchbearer.

Scene 5

Shylock has had a bad dream about money. He has been invited to dine with Bassanio and instructs Jessica to shut up the house and ignore the music and noise.

Scene 6

Lorenzo and Jessica meet up. She has the money and jewels. Suddenly Antonio decides Bassanio and Gratiano must go aboard. The wind has changed.

Scene 7

At Belmont, the Prince of Morocco talks his way through all three caskets and chooses gold. It is the wrong one. Portia is not disappointed.

Scene 8

Solanio has seen Shylock in the streets, who has learnt that his daughter has left. Two bags of ducats and some precious jewels have gone with her. She is planning to marry a Christian. There is a rumour that a ship has been wrecked in the waters between England and France. They fear it may be one of Antonio's.

Scene 9

At Belmont, the Prince of Arragon is about to choose a casket. After much debate he chooses silver. As he leaves, Bassanio is about to arrive.

Act 3

Scene 1

There is still rumour that one of Antonio's ships is wrecked. Shylock is upset about his daughter's departure. He has heard of Antonio's loss and his anger at Antonio is considerable. Shylock pleads that as a Jew, he too is human. A friend of Shylock's, Tubal, has tried to find Jessica without success. She has spent money and bought a monkey with a ring. Shylock would rather his daughter were dead. The rumour now is that Antonio must break his bond. Shylock insists he will have Antonio's heart.

Scene 2

Bassanio is at the point of choosing a casket. Portia asks him to delay as she doesn't want to lose him. Bassanio chooses lead – the correct one. They are both delighted. Nerissa and Gratiano have also decided to marry. That too depended on Bassanio's choice. Salerio arrives with a letter. As Bassanio reads it, Portia can see that it contains seriously bad news. Bassanio now has to admit he has no money and is in debt to Antonio. It appears that all Antonio's ventures have failed. Shylock will demand Antonio's flesh rather than accept any amount of money. Portia immediately offers all the money that might save Antonio. She and Bassanio marry. Bassanio leaves to go to Venice.

Scene 3

Antonio is put in gaol. He knows there is no hope for him. Shylock continues to demand his bond. Even the Duke will not be able to alter the law of Venice. Too much depends on it.

Scene 4

Lorenzo and Jessica arrive at Belmont. Lorenzo praises Portia for letting Bassanio go to Antonio. She tells Lorenzo that she and Nerissa will spend time at a monastery until he returns. She asks Lorenzo and Jessica to look after her house while she is away. When this settled Portia sends a messenger to a lawyer, Doctor Bellario. Portia intends that she and Nerissa will dress as men and play a part. They leave in her coach.

Scene 5

Launcelot jokes with Jessica. Lorenzo and Jessica quite enjoy their role and Launcelot's clowning. He and Jessica go in to dinner.

Act 4

Scene 1

The Duke visits Antonio, who knows that nothing can be done to help him. The Duke addresses Shylock who will not change his mind, Bassanio and the Duke continue to address Shylock. Portia and Nerissa appear as lawyer and clerk, while Shylock sharpens his knife. Portia speaks to both Shylock and Antonio, then speaks of mercy. Portia appears to plead with Shylock, then makes it plain that it is right that he must have his bond. He is very pleased with her.

Portia calls for scales. The weight of flesh must be one pound, no more, no less, and no blood must be spilled. If it is, Shylock will suffer severe penalties. When Shylock hears this he thinks he will take the money, but it is too late for that. He has tried to take the life of a citizen of the state. Therefore half of his goods must go to Antonio, the other half to the state. The Duke can decide not to take his life and does pardon him. Antonio decides he wants to leave Shylock with half his goods. He'll take the other half for Lorenzo and Jessica when her father dies. Shylock must also convert to Christianity. Shylock is a broken man.

As the lawyer and clerk, the only grateful gifts that Portia and Nerissa will accept are the rings they gave their husbands. The men part with them very reluctantly.

Act 5

Scene 1

When Portia and Nerissa arrive back at Belmont they soon confront their husbands' 'betrayal'. They suggest the missing rings were given to women. They clear up the misunderstandings. Lorenzo and Jessica are delighted to learn of their future fortune, and Antonio discovers that three of his ships have come safely to harbour after all.

Background to the play

Date of the play

Scholars have suggested that Shakespeare wrote *The Merchant of Venice* some time between the late summer of 1596 and 1598. The evidence for this depends on detective work.

After several setbacks in the war against Spain, the Earl of Essex planned a naval expedition to attack and capture the Spanish port of Cadiz. There were 93 English and 18 Dutch ships that sailed from Plymouth in June 1596. Three weeks later they made a surprise attack on Cadiz, which was undefended. The Spaniards were burning their own ships to prevent their capture, but the English seized the *San Matias* and *San Andres* and took them back to England.

The *San Andres*, a splendid ship, was renamed the *Andrew*. The ship made several well-publicised voyages but it does not seem likely that it would have become generally recognised as the symbol of a rich trading ship until the following year. This dating is based on line 27 in Act 1 scene 1: 'And see my wealthy Andrew docked in sand'.

So the likelihood is that *The Merchant of Venice* went into the repertory of the Lord Chamberlain's Men (Shakespeare's theatre company) in the 1597 season. The first performance of the play is not likely to have been later than 1598 because that is the date given for its appearance in a register of published plays. Plays were not usually printed until after their first successful season on the stage.

Plot and characters

Shakespeare is believed to have taken the story of this play from an Italian short story of the late fourteenth century. The scene is set in Venice and at Belmont. The Lady of Belmont sets a different task for her suitors, but the other elements are very similar to Shakespeare's play. The young man who eventually wins the lady has lost valuable ships before, his benefactor (in the short story, his godfather) has to pledge a pound of flesh to a Jewish money-lender. When the bond falls due, the lady offers ten times the pledge. When the Jew refuses, she comes to court in disguise, as Portia does, and wins. The story of the rings is there too.

Shakespeare adds the story of the caskets, gives his Jew a daughter and leaves Antonio unmarried.

There is also a suggestion that Shakespeare was competing with a very popular play *The Jew of Malta* written in 1589 by Christopher Marlowe. This play treats the Jew, called Barabas, as a thoroughly evil villain, a wicked ogre. Shakespeare is not entirely free from the idea that usurer = Jew = evil, but he does allow us to see Shylock as a human being who has himself been wronged.

Jews in England

In theory, only Jews who had converted to Christianity were allowed to live in England in Shakespeare's day. Jews who practised their own religion were banned from England in 1290 and only readmitted by Oliver Cromwell in the seventeenth century.

The year after his early death in 1593, Marlowe's play became even more popular. In 1594 Queen Elizabeth I's doctor was executed for high treason. He was a Portuguese Jew, Dr Roderigo Lopez, who had converted to Christianity 35 years previously and was a fashionable society doctor in London. The charge against him was that he had plotted to poison Queen Elizabeth. This was doubted then and is now, but there was much public prejudice against him as he was both a foreigner and a Jew.

What does seem clear is that he was a spy for the English in their dealings with Spain and Portugal, and almost certainly a double-agent – a dangerous trade. He was hanged, drawn and quartered, and people flocked to Marlowe's play.

Anti-Semitism

In his book *Anti-Semitism: The Longest Hatred*, Robert S. Wistrich traces the origins of anti-Semitism to pagan times. Simplified, he believes the main elements are:

- When, in the third century BCE, some Jews moved out of the Holy Land to Greece and Rome, they did not intermingle with non-Jews (Gentiles); they kept to their belief in one God; they preserved their laws on what food they were allowed to eat; they maintained their separate lifestyle and above all their pride in being God's chosen people.
- The resentment this pattern of behaviour caused soon became mixed with myth and superstition, including the accusation of ritual murder. Historians started to write about this as though it were fact. Because Jews kept to themselves they were accused of being unpatriotic, and 'haters of mankind'.
- By contrast, in the first century CE was the Jews' insistence that they were superior to the 'heathen' around them. They attempted to convert people to the Jewish religion and were successful. Thus at the beginning of the Christian era in the Roman Empire there were some ten million Jews (10–12 per cent of the total population). Of course this success also caused resentment, as did their success in business and in learning, which brought them wealth, power and privilege.
- Jesus was born, lived and died as a Jew in first-century Roman Palestine. So did his parents and his disciples. So early Christianity was born out of Judaism.
- Jesus was crucified by the occupying power, Rome, as a troublesome Jewish agitator. However, Wistrich claims the story of the death of Jesus as told in the New Testament shifts responsibility for his crucifixion from the Romans to the Jews. This, the killing of the son of God, is the most frequently given 'reason' today for hatred of Jewish people.

Prejudice

Throughout the centuries, Jews have been subjected to massacres and to forced conversion to Christianity; they have been outlawed from several European countries; and they have been made to live in ghettos – a part of the town reserved for them.

It is impossible to give a reason for prejudice because there is no 'reason' for it. There is no 'reason' for bullying or for wars of religion. The sad fact is that people are easily frightened and feel threatened by what seems strange to them and by what they can't be bothered to try to understand. This includes, of course, different skin colour, different language, different culture, different habits, different beliefs – anything seen as 'different', in fact.

People in power have often found this very useful. Hitler, for instance, with continuous propaganda for many years, managed to persuade his public that most of their troubles would be solved if they could get rid of the Jews.

His task was made easier by the fact that he could invent 'an international conspiracy' as part of his racist plan, because most countries in the world today have Jews as their citizens. For his extermination programme to succeed, however, he needed to make the victims seem 'non-human'. Tolerance disappears when people forget that everyone, whatever their race, religion or colour, feels just the same if hurt, either by words, or by physical violence.

Shakespeare's theatre

Nowadays entertainment is piped into people's houses – TV, the internet and radio provide hundreds of different programme choices every day. But in Shakespeare's time, people went out to be entertained. If you lived in a city like London you could go to the theatre.

But it wasn't the kind of theatre we know today. There was no electricity and the only artificial lighting was candles or torches, so plays had to be watched in daylight. This meant that the main part of the theatre was open to the skies.

Many of Shakespeare's plays were performed at the Globe Theatre. A modern replica of the Globe now stands on London's Bankside, close to where the original was built. By visiting the Globe Theatre you can discover what it was like to go to the theatre in Shakespeare's time.

Once you were inside, you would see that the ground plan was more or less circular: in *Henry V*, Shakespeare talks about 'the wooden O'. All around the outside were galleries where people could pay to sit on a wooden bench. From the galleries you looked down on the stage and – very important – you were under cover if it rained!

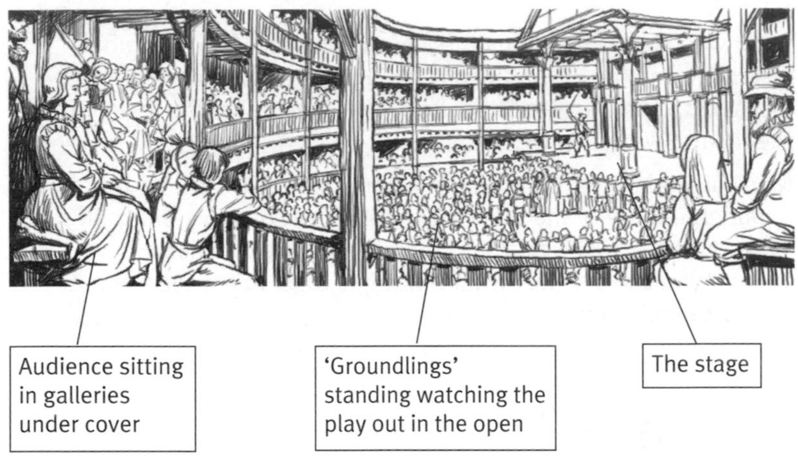

The stage measured about 12 metres by 12 metres. It was raised about 1.5 metres above the ground and was surrounded by a wide standing area. This was where the 'groundlings' went to watch the play. It was the cheapest way of seeing a play, but it meant that you had to stand for anything up to three hours. On the other hand, you were much closer to the action – the people at the front were close enough to touch the actors when they came to the edge of the stage.

As you will see when you read the play, Shakespeare often gives the characters **soliloquies**, speeches which they make when alone on stage. Often they seem to be deliberately sharing their thoughts with the audience. When you look at the stage of the Globe and see how close the audience was, you realise how effective this must have been.

Some modern theatres have a curtain which hides the stage from the audience before the play and between scenes. This makes it easy to change the scenery without the audience seeing what is going on. In Shakespeare's theatre there was no curtain to conceal the main stage; the stage was always open to the audience. Very little scenery was used and if furniture was needed, the actors had to carry it on themselves. Similarly, if a character died on stage, the body had to be carried off as part of the action.

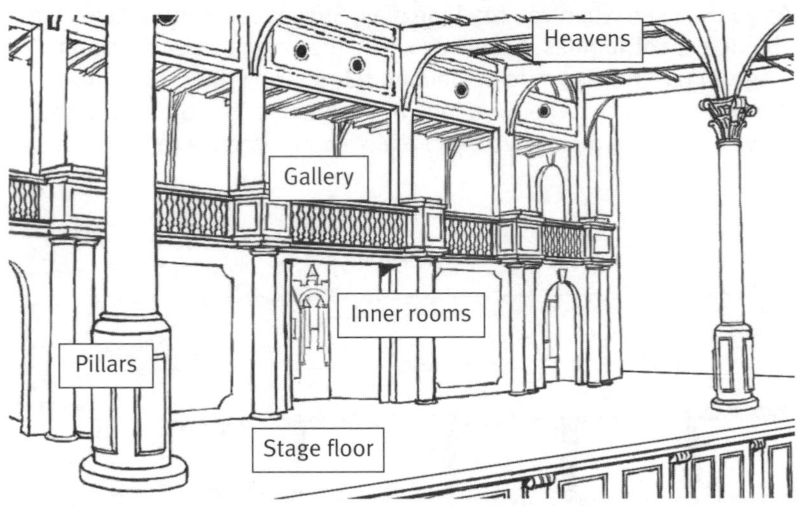

The stage was, however, quite complicated. Two large pillars on the main lower stage supported the roof, which was known as the 'heavens'. This kept the actors dry if it rained, but it could also be used for the action of the play. In some of the plays, Shakespeare has characters lowered from above down onto the stage. There were also trapdoors in the stage itself, so that people could suddenly appear from below. The heavens contained a space which could be used for sound effects. Cannons could be fired for battle scenes and cannon balls rolled along the floor to make the sound of thunder. At the back of the stage there was an inner room which could be concealed by a curtain. This was sometimes used for short scenes in the play.

Shakespeare's language

It is easy to look at the text of this play and say to yourself, 'I'm never going to understand that!' but it is important not to be put off. Remember that there are two reasons why Shakespeare's language may seem strange at first:

1 He was writing 400 years ago and the English language has changed over the centuries.

2 He wrote mainly in **verse**. As a result he sometimes changed the order of words to make them fit the verse form, and he used a large number of 'tricks of the trade': figures of speech and other techniques.

Language change

This can cause three main kinds of problem:

Grammar

Since the end of the sixteenth century there have been some changes in English grammar. Some examples:

1 *Thee*, *thou*, *thy*, and the verb forms that go with them are used alongside *you*, *your*.

JESSICA	Who are *you*? Tell me for more certainty, Albeit I swear that I do know *your* tongue.
LORENZO	Lorenzo and *thy* love.

Thou is usually used from master to servant:

BASSANIO	I know thee well, *thou hast* obtained *thy* suit. Shylock *thy* master spoke with me this day And *hath* preferred thee...

2 Words contract (shorten) in different ways. For example: '*tis* rather than *it's*; *ne'er* for *never*.

3 Some of the 'little words' are different. For example: *an* for *if*, *ay* for *yes*, *twain* for *two*.

Words that have changed their meaning

Sometimes you will come across words that you think you know, but discover that they don't mean what you expect them to mean. For example: *naughty* (Act 3 scene 3 line 9) meant 'wicked' or 'worthless' in Shakespeare's day. Now it means 'disobedient' or 'badly behaved'. In the same line *fond* now suggests affection. Then it meant 'foolish'.

Words that have gone out of use

These are the most obvious and most frequent causes of difficulty. Shakespeare had – and used – a huge vocabulary. He loved using words, and pushing them to their limits. So you will come across many words you have not met before. They are usually explained in the notes on the page facing the text.

The language of the play

Most of *The Merchant of Venice* is in **blank verse** – 'blank' because these lines do not rhyme. Parts of the play are in **prose** and short sections are in rhymed verse.

Blank verse

The main part of the play is written in **iambic pentameter** – lines of ten syllables with a repeated pattern of weak and strong beats:

*Thou **art** too **wild**, too **rude** and **bold** of **voice***
(ti **tum** ti **tum** ti **tum** ti **tum** ti **tum**)

If Shakespeare had given every line exactly the same **rhythm** the play would soon become very monotonous, so he varies the rhythm in a number of ways. Sometimes lines are not exactly ten syllables long or are divided between two or more characters. Often he just changes the pattern of weak and strong beats slightly:

Why** doth the **Jew pause**? **Take** thy **for**fei**ture
(**tum** ti ti **tum tum tum** ti **tum** ti **tum**)

But this line, at a turning point in the play, also has one extra strong beat, and a deliberate pause for effect in the middle of the line, called the **caesura** (see Glossary p. 238).

Shakespeare also expected the actors to speak his lines in a natural manner, not pausing at the end of each line unless the sense of the words made it necessary. The need to pause at the commas, semi-colons and dashes show Portia's hesitations and confusions as she tries to keep Bassanio with her as long as she can:

PORTIA I pray you tarry, pause a day or two
Before you hazard, for in choosing wrong
I lose your company; therefore forbear awhile.
There's something tells me – but it is not love –
I would not lose you, and you know yourself
Hate counsels not in such a quality.

Portia has been sure that she does not even like any of the suitors she has met so far. Suddenly she finds she is in love with Bassanio. She must not say so, but she can't help it. She has taken an oath to marry the man who makes the right choice of casket but she must not hint at the right answer. She wants Bassanio to make the choice that will win her, but she is afraid he will fail and she will lose him forever.

Rhymed verse

Sometimes Shakespeare uses a pattern of rhymed lines. It may be just two successive lines, known as a rhyming couplet:

PORTIA How all the other passions fleet to **air**,
As doubtful thoughts, and rash-embraced des**pair**

Such couplets are often used to round off a scene. Sometimes characters who exit one after the other each have a rhyming couplet.

SHYLOCK Fast bind, fast **find**,
A proverb never stale in thrifty **mind**. [*Exit*

JESSICA Farewell, and if my fortune be not **crossed**,
I have a father, you a daughter **lost**. [*Exit*

Sometimes the pattern of rhyme varies. When Bassanio, just married, leaves on his apparently hopeless mission to free Antonio, the leave-taking is more formal and ceremonious:

BASSANIO Since I have your good leave to go **away**,
I will make haste; but till I come again,
No bed shall e'er be guilty of my **stay**,
Nor rest be interposer 'twixt us twain.

The need for ceremony and a 'rounded' end to the situation produces rhymed verses on the scrolls which the losers – and the winner – find in the three caskets.

Prose

Some of the play is written in prose, i.e. ordinary sentences. If you look at the play as a whole, you will see that prose is used for certain characters and situations. Shakespeare's comic characters do not use verse (unless they are acting in a play within a play). In Act 2 scene 2 Launcelot is trying to decide his future. He is talking to himself, and does not use verse here, or in jokey conversation with his aged father, or when asking Bassanio for a job. In Act 1 scene 3 (lines 14–26) where Shylock is considering the loan, he works out the risks in prose. Where there is strong emotion – in scenes where characters are expressing their love (Act 3 scene 2) or in the drama of the scenes in court (Act 4 scene 1) blank verse is appropriate.

The Merchant of Venice

Characters

THE DUKE OF VENICE

THE PRINCE OF MOROCCO, THE PRINCE OF ARRAGON } suitors to Portia

ANTONIO, a merchant of Venice

BASSANIO, his friend, suitor to Portia

SOLANIO, SALERIO, GRATIANO } friends to Antonio and Bassanio

LORENZO, in love with Jessica

SHYLOCK, a rich Jew

TUBAL, a Jew, his friend

LAUNCELOT GOBBO, a clown, servant to Shylock

OLD GOBBO, father to Launcelot

LEONARDO, servant to Bassanio

BALTHASAR, STEPHANO } servants to Portia

PORTIA, an heiress

NERISSA, her waiting-woman

JESSICA, daughter to Shylock

Magnificoes of Venice, Officers of the Court of Justice, Gaoler, Musicians, Servants, and other Attendants

Scene: *Venice, and Portia's house at Belmont*

Antonio, a merchant, tells his friends he feels sad without knowing why. They say he is concerned about his ships and cargoes.

1 **sooth** truth

4 **whereof ... born** what causes it

5 **I am to learn** I don't yet know

6–7 **such ... myself** it puts me in such a senseless state of sadness that I scarcely know who or what I am

9 **argosies** large merchant ships

portly sail sails swollen by the wind

10 **signors ... burghers** gentlemen and rich citizens (well fed and so 'portly')

11 **pageants** carnival floats

12 **overpeer** tower above and look down on

petty traffickers small merchant ships

13 **curtsy** bob about

do them reverence bow to them

14 **woven wings** sails

15 **venture** A business investment with the chance of making more money but the risk of losing the money put in.

16 **The better part** most

17 **still** all the time

18 **Plucking the grass** picking a blade of grass and holding it up to see which way the wind is blowing

19 **roads** i.e. sheltered waters near the shore where ships can anchor safely

22 **wind** breath

broth soup

23 **ague** fever, shivering fit from fever or fear

26 **flats** mud flats; invisible under water and so dangerous to ships

Act One

Scene 1

Venice

Enter ANTONIO, SALERIO, *and* SOLANIO

ANTONIO In sooth I know not why I am so sad.
It wearies me, you say it wearies you;
But how I caught it, found it, or came by it,
What stuff 'tis made of, whereof it is born,
I am to learn.
And such a want-wit sadness makes of me,
That I have much ado to know myself.

SALERIO Your mind is tossing on the ocean,
There, where your argosies with portly sail,
Like signors and rich burghers on the flood,
Or as it were the pageants of the sea,
Do overpeer the petty traffickers
That curtsy to them, do them reverence,
As they fly by them with their woven wings.

SOLANIO Believe me, sir, had I such venture forth,
The better part of my affections would
Be with my hopes abroad. I should be still
Plucking the grass to know where sits the wind,
Peering in maps for ports and piers and roads;
And every object that might make me fear
Misfortune to my ventures, out of doubt
Would make me sad.

SALERIO My wind, cooling my broth,
Would blow me to an ague when I thought
What harm a wind too great might do at sea.
I should not see the sandy hour-glass run,
But I should think of shallows and of flats,

Antonio assures them he has no need to worry about his ships. He rejects the suggestion that he might be in love.

27 **Andrew** Usually taken to refer to a real Spanish ship, the San Andres, which the English captured at Cadiz in 1596 and took into their fleet.

28 **Vailing** lowering, letting down

high-top topsail

29 **burial** grave

Should I go If I were to go

30 **edifice** building

31 **bethink me** be reminded of

straight immediately

32 **gentle** noble, excellent

33 **stream** ocean

34 **Enrobe** dress

35 **but ... this** a moment ago so valuable

36–8 **Shall I ... sad?** Is it possible that I should have these thoughts without realising I would feel sad if such things actually happened?

39 **tell not me** don't bother to tell me

42 **ventures** enterprises

bottom ship

44 **Upon** at risk on

46 **Fie, fie!** (an exclamation of dismay or disgust)

50 **two-headed Janus** the Roman god, who guarded gates and doors (He was supposed to have two faces, one at the back of his head. He gives his name to the month of January.)

51 **framed** made

52 **peep** glance

54 **vinegar aspect** sour expression

56 **Nestor** the name of an old Greek general at the siege of Troy (It is used here to mean a wise old man.)

jest joke

And see my wealthy Andrew docked in sand,
Vailing her high-top lower than her ribs
To kiss her burial. Should I go to church
And see the holy edifice of stone,
And not bethink me straight of dangerous rocks,
Which touching but my gentle vessel's side
Would scatter all her spices on the stream,
Enrobe the roaring waters with my silks,
And, in a word, but even now worth this,
And now worth nothing? Shall I have the thought
To think on this, and shall I lack the thought
That such a thing bechanced would make me sad?
But tell not me, I know Antonio
Is sad to think upon his merchandise.

ANTONIO Believe me no, I thank my fortune for it,
My ventures are not in one bottom trusted,
Nor to one place; nor is my whole estate
Upon the fortune of this present year.
Therefore my merchandise makes me not sad.

SOLANIO Why then you are in love.

ANTONIO Fie, fie!

SOLANIO Not in love neither: then let us say you are sad
Because you are not merry; and 'twere as easy
For you to laugh and leap and say you are merry
Because you are not sad. Now by two-headed
Janus,
Nature hath framed strange fellows in her time:
Some that will evermore peep through their eyes
And laugh like parrots at a bagpiper;
And other of such vinegar aspect
That they'll not show their teeth in way of smile
Though Nestor swear the jest be laughable.

Enter BASSANIO, LORENZO, *and* GRATIANO

Here comes Bassanio your most noble kinsman,
Gratiano, and Lorenzo. Fare ye well,

When Salerio and Solanio have left, Gratiano comments on Antonio's unhappy state, and starts to give Antonio advice.

64 **embrace th'occasion** take the chance

66 **when ... laugh?** when shall we meet to enjoy some time together?

67 **exceeding strange** very aloof, distant

68 **We'll ... yours** We'll find a time that suits you.

74 **You ... world** you care too much for people's opinion

75 **They ... care** It is not worth having if it takes so much effort

80 **With ... come** there must be wrinkles in old age but they should be caused by laughter

81 **liver** The liver was thought to be the part of the body responsible for passion.

82 **mortifying** deadly

84 **Sit ... alabaster** sit bent like an old man carved in white marble

85 **jaundice** a disease which shows as yellowish skin

86 **peevish** obstinate

89 **Do ... pond** look like scum or algae on a stagnant pond

90 **do ... entertain** obstinately keep silent

We leave you now with better company.

SALERIO I would have stayed till I had made you merry,
If worthier friends had not prevented me.

ANTONIO Your worth is very dear in my regard.
I take it your own business calls on you,
And you embrace th'occasion to depart.

SALERIO Good morrow my good lords.

BASSANIO Good signors both, when shall we laugh? Say, when?
You grow exceeding strange. Must it be so?

SALERIO We'll make our leisures to attend on yours.

[*Exeunt* SALERIO *and* SOLANIO

LORENZO My Lord Bassanio, since you have found Antonio,
We two will leave you, but at dinner-time
I pray you have in mind where we must meet.

BASSANIO I will not fail you.

GRATIANO You look not well Signior Antonio,
You have too much respect upon the world,
They lose it that do buy it with much care;
Believe me you are marvellously changed.

ANTONIO I hold the world but as the world, Gratiano,
A stage where every man must play a part,
And mine a sad one.

GRATIANO Let me play the fool;
With mirth and laughter let old wrinkles come,
And let my liver rather heat with wine
Than my heart cool with mortifying groans.
Why should a man whose blood is warm within
Sit like his grandsire, cut in alabaster?
Sleep when he wakes? And creep into the jaundice
By being peevish? I tell thee what Antonio –
I love thee, and it is my love that speaks –
There are a sort of men whose visages
Do cream and mantle like a standing pond,
And do a wilful stillness entertain,

Gratiano continues to warn Antonio not to adopt a false pose of silence, in order to be regarded as a wise man. Antonio and Bassanio are finally left alone. Bassanio has promised to reveal to Antonio the name of the lady he wishes to visit.

91 **With ... opinion** so that people think they have an opinion

93 **Sir Oracle** wisdom itself

94 **ope** open

98 **damn** condemn (possibly with a **pun** on 'dam' = 'stop up')

101–2 **fish ... opinion** do not hope to attract men's good opinion by posing as a silent melancholy man; such an opinion is not worth having

102 **gudgeon** a small fish, thought to be easy to catch

104 **exhortation** speech

108 **moe** more, longer

110 **gear** this kind of talk

112 **neat's tongue dried** cured ox tongue

vendible saleable, likely to be marriageable

115 **reasons** explanations

120 **pilgrimage** This word is usually reserved for a journey to places of great importance to world religions, or to the shrine of a saint.

123–5 **How ... continuance** how much money I have spent displaying a higher standard of living than my small income could continue to support

With purpose to be dressed in an opinion
Of wisdom, gravity, profound conceit,
As who should say, 'I am Sir Oracle,
And when I ope my lips let no dog bark.'
O my Antonio, I do know of these
That therefore only are reputed wise
For saying nothing; when I am very sure
If they should speak, would almost damn those ears,
Which hearing them would call their brothers fools.
I'll tell thee more of this another time.
But fish not with this melancholy bait
For this fool gudgeon, this opinion.
Come good Lorenzo. Fare ye well awhile,
I'll end my exhortation after dinner.

LORENZO Well, we will leave you then till dinner-time.
I must be one of these same dumb wise men,
For Gratiano never lets me speak.

GRATIANO Well, keep me company but two years moe,
Thou shalt not know the sound of thine own tongue.

ANTONIO Fare you well: I'll grow a talker for this gear.

GRATIANO Thanks i'faith, for silence is only commendable
In a neat's tongue dried, and a maid not vendible.

[*Exeunt* GRATIANO *and* LORENZO

ANTONIO Is that anything now?

BASSANIO Gratiano speaks an infinite deal of nothing, more than any man in all Venice. His reasons are as two grains of wheat hid in two bushels of chaff: you shall seek all day ere you find them, and when you have them, they are not worth the search.

ANTONIO Well, tell me now what lady is the same
To whom you swore a secret pilgrimage,
That you today promised to tell me of?

BASSANIO 'Tis not unknown to you Antonio,
How much I have disabled mine estate,
By something showing a more swelling port

Bassanio acknowledges that he has been living above his income. He owes most to Antonio, but asks him to lend still more in the hope of getting at least some of it back. Antonio promises all he has.

126–7 **Nor ... rate** neither am I complaining now at having to cut down on my high spending

127 **care** concern

come fairly off discharge honourably

129 **my time** my youth

something too prodigal rather too wasteful

130 **gaged** tangled

132 **from ... warranty** because I know you love me, I am able

136–7 **And ... honour** if it (the plan) is honourable as you yourself always are

138 **extremest means** all my wealth

139 **Lie ... occasions** are all available to meet your needs

140 **shaft** arrow

141 **fellow ... flight** another, identical arrow (The 'flight' is the particular pattern of feathers on the arrow that determines how the arrow will fly.)

142 **advised** careful

144 **urge** insist on

148 **self** same

150–1 **or ... Or** either ... or

151 **latter hazard** second amount of money risked

152 **rest** remain

153–4 **herein ... circumstance** by speaking like this, you are wasting time appealing to my affection in such a roundabout way

156 **making ... uttermost** doubting I would do the very most I could

160 **prest unto it** ready to do it, committed to it

Than my faint means would grant continuance;
Nor do I now make moan to be abridged
From such a noble rate, but my chief care
Is to come fairly off from the great debts
Wherein my time, something too prodigal,
Hath left me gaged. To you Antonio
I owe the most in money and in love,
And from your love I have a warranty
To unburden all my plots and purposes
How to get clear of all the debts I owe.

ANTONIO I pray you good Bassanio let me know it,
And if it stand as you yourself still do,
Within the eye of honour, be assured
My purse, my person, my extremest means
Lie all unlocked to your occasions.

BASSANIO In my school days, when I had lost one shaft,
I shot his fellow of the selfsame flight
The selfsame way, with more advised watch
To find the other forth, and by adventuring both
I oft found both. I urge this childhood proof
Because what follows is pure innocence.
I owe you much, and like a wilful youth,
That which I owe is lost, but if you please
To shoot another arrow that self way
Which you did shoot the first, I do not doubt,
As I will watch the aim, or to find both,
Or bring your latter hazard back again,
And thankfully rest debtor for the first.

ANTONIO You know me well, and herein spend but time
To wind about my love with circumstance;
And out of doubt you do me now more wrong
In making question of my uttermost
Than if you had made waste of all I have.
Then do but say to me what I should do
That in your knowledge may by me be done,
And I am prest unto it. Therefore speak.

Bassanio now needs money to equip himself to go to Belmont as a suitor for Portia, a rich and beautiful heiress, whom many men wish to marry. Antonio does not have the cash at present, but promises him the money – if he is able to borrow it.

161 **richly left** a rich heiress

162 **fair** beautiful (and also with a fair complexion)

fairer … word even more than that word implies

163 **virtues** qualities

165 **nothing undervalued** not inferior in value; Portia was the name of the daughter of Cato, a Roman statesman, general, and opponent of Caesar. Married to Brutus, one of the conspirators who murdered Caesar, she was highly thought of for her loyalty and love for her husband, and her intelligence and learning.

169 **Renowned** famous

170–2 **golden fleece/Colchos/Jason** In Greek myth, Jason gathered together a crew for the ship Argos in which they sailed through dangerous seas to fetch the golden fleece from Colchis. It was guarded by a fierce dragon but Medea, the daughter of the King of Colchis, helped them to win it and escape with it and her. However, she had used witchcraft and the story ended in tragedy.

171 **seat** estate

Colchos' strand the country of Colchis: the eastern end of the Black Sea, in modern day Georgia

175 **presages … thrift** foretells such success for me

178 **commodity** goods

179 **present sum** instant cash

181 **racked** stretched (as on the rack, an instrument of torture)

182 **To … Portia** to fit you out to visit the beautiful Portia at Belmont

183 **presently** straight away

185 **of … sake** on my credit or out of regard for me

4 **in … abundance as** as many as

BASSANIO In Belmont is a lady richly left,
And she is fair, and fairer than that word,
Of wondrous virtues – sometimes from her eyes
I did receive fair speechless messages.
Her name is Portia, nothing undervalued
To Cato's daughter, Brutus' Portia.
Nor is the wide world ignorant of her worth,
For the four winds blow in from every coast
Renowned suitors, and her sunny locks
Hang on her temples like a golden fleece,
Which makes her seat of Belmont Colchos' strand,
And many Jasons come in quest of her.
O my Antonio, had I but the means
To hold a rival place with one of them,
I have a mind presages me such thrift,
That I should questionless be fortunate.

ANTONIO Thou know'st that all my fortunes are at sea,
Neither have I money nor commodity
To raise a present sum. Therefore go forth;
Try what my credit can in Venice do,
That shall be racked even to the uttermost
To furnish thee to Belmont to fair Portia.
Go presently inquire, and so will I,
Where money is, and I no question make
To have it of my trust, or for my sake.

[*Exeunt*

Scene 2

Belmont

Enter PORTIA *and* NERISSA

PORTIA By my troth Nerissa, my little body is aweary of this great world.

NERISSA You would be, sweet madam, if your miseries were in the same abundance as your good fortunes are;

In his will, Portia's father has decreed that she must marry the man who makes the correct choice between three caskets, of gold, silver and lead. Portia finds this hard to take. Nerissa tries to reassure her. They start to discuss the suitors so far.

5 **for ... see** as far as I can see

surfeit are overfilled

7 **mean** small

8 **mean** middle area

superfluity ... hairs excess soon makes people seem old

9 **competency** moderation

10 **sentences** 1) wise sayings 2) court judgements

pronounced 1) expressed 2) handed down by a judge

14 **divine** priest

17–20 **The brain ... cripple** Portia is saying that although it is easy for the brain to work out what the body should do, a rush of emotions often takes over, making good advice look wrong. She uses the parallel of the hare, which seems to act crazily at mating time, managing to avoid the nets set to trap it.

21 **reasoning** discussion

in the fashion of a kind

24 **will** 1) wishes 2) the will left by her father

28–33 **the lottery ... love** the lottery of the three caskets means that the person who gets the right answer wins your hand and it is certain that the man who does win will be the man who truly loves you

36 **over-name them** run through their names

38 **level** make a guess

40 **colt** young horse (i.e. young inexperienced lad)

and yet for aught I see, they are as sick that surfeit with too much, as they that starve with nothing. It is no mean happiness therefore to be seated in the mean; superfluity comes sooner by white hairs, but competency lives longer.

PORTIA Good sentences, and well pronounced.

NERISSA They would be better if well followed.

PORTIA If to do were as easy as to know what were good to do, chapels had been churches, and poor men's cottages princes' palaces. It is a good divine that follows his own instructions. I can easier teach twenty what were good to be done, than be one of the twenty to follow mine own teaching. The brain may devise laws for the blood, but a hot temper leaps o'er a cold decree; such a hare is madness the youth, to skip o'er the meshes of good counsel the cripple. But this reasoning is not in the fashion to choose me a husband. O me, the word 'choose'! I may neither choose whom I would, nor refuse whom I dislike; so is the will of a living daughter curbed by the will of a dead father. Is it not hard Nerissa, that I cannot choose one, nor refuse none?

NERISSA Your father was ever virtuous, and holy men at their death have good inspirations, therefore the lottery that he hath devised in these three chests of gold, silver, and lead, whereof who chooses his meaning chooses you, will no doubt never be chosen by any rightly, but one who you shall rightly love. But what warmth is there in your affection towards any of these princely suitors that are already come?

PORTIA I pray thee over-name them, and as thou namest them, I will describe them, and, according to my description level at my affection.

NERISSA First there is the Neapolitan prince.

PORTIA Ay, that's a colt indeed, for he doth nothing but

Portia says what she thinks of her suitors: the horsey man from Naples, the miserable German Count, the show-off French Lord, and the badly dressed Englishman with no foreign languages. (These opinions are largely in line with the stereotypical views of other nationalities common in Shakespeare's time.)

42 **appropriation ... parts** advantage to his own personality

43 **afeard** afraid

44 **smith** blacksmith

45 **County** Count

46 **as who** like someone saying

An If

48–9 **weeping philosopher** A Greek philosopher Heracleitus wept at the whole spectacle of human life, and so was known by this title.

51 **death's-head** skull

60 **he ... no man** he seems to be all possible men at once

61 **throstle** thrush

a-capering leaping around

65 **requite him** repay his attentions

69 **hath** (here) speaks

72 **proper man's picture** a handsome man to look at

74 **suited** dressed

75 **round hose** very full short breeches

bonnet cap

76 **behaviour everywhere** She finds his behaviour strange and completely foreign to her.

talk of his horse, and he makes it a great appropriation to his own good parts that he can shoe him himself. I am much afeared my lady his mother played false with a smith.

NERISSA Then there is the County Palatine.

PORTIA He doth nothing but frown, as who should say 'An you will not have me, choose'; he hears merry tales and smiles not; I fear he will prove the weeping philosopher when he grows old, being so full of unmannerly sadness in his youth. I had rather be married to a death's-head with a bone in his mouth than to either of these. God defend me from these two.

NERISSA How say you by the French lord, Monsieur Le Bon?

PORTIA God made him, and therefore let him pass for a man. In truth I know it is a sin to be a mocker, but he – why he hath a horse better than the Neapolitan's, a better bad habit of frowning than the Count Palatine; he is every man in no man; if a throstle sing, he falls straight a-capering; he will fence with his own shadow. If I should marry him, I should marry twenty husbands. If he would despise me, I would forgive him, for if he love me to madness, I shall never requite him.

NERISSA What say you then to Falconbridge, the young baron of England?

PORTIA You know I say nothing to him, for he understands not me, nor I him: he hath neither Latin, French, nor Italian and you will come into the court and swear that I have a poor pennyworth in the English. He is a proper man's picture, but alas, who can converse with a dumb show? How oddly he is suited! I think he bought his doublet in Italy, his round hose in France, his bonnet in Germany, and his behaviour everywhere.

The list continues: the Scotsman who hates the English, and the young German who likes his drink. Nerissa reveals that the six suitors have all decided to go home without making the choice of the caskets. Portia is determined to abide by her father's will.

78 **neighbourly charity** the kindness of a neighbour

78–82 **That ... another** Portia comments with humour on the aggression between the Scotsman and the Englishman, using 'borrow' and 'pay back' for the blows and saying that the Frenchman guaranteed another box on the ear.

79 **borrowed ... ear** the Englishman hit him

82 **sealed under** set his seal on it

85 **vilely** horribly

88 **beast** animal

88–90 **An ... him** If the worst comes to the worst, Portia will do her best to do without him.

91–93 **If ... him** If he decides to choose and chooses the right casket, you will be breaking your oath if you then decide to reject him

95 **Rhenish wine** a white wine from the Rhine area

98 **a sponge** i.e. someone who mops up drink like a sponge

103 **by ... sort** in some other way

104 **your father's imposition** the conditions your father set

105 **Sibylla** In Greek and Roman legend the sibyls foretold the future. The sibyl of Cumae asked Apollo for the gift of long life.

106 **Diana** the moon-goddess (portrayed as a huntress and protector of virgins)

107 **parcel** group

108–9 **I dote on** I am head-over-heels in love with

NERISSA What think you of the Scottish lord his neighbour?

PORTIA That he hath a neighbourly charity in him, for he borrowed a box of the ear of the Englishman, and swore he would pay him again when he was able. I think the Frenchman became his surety and sealed under for another.

NERISSA How like you the young German, the Duke of Saxony's nephew?

PORTIA Very vilely in the morning when he is sober, and most vilely in the afternoon when he is drunk. When he is best, he is a little worse than a man, and when he is worst, he is little better than a beast. An the worst fall that ever fell, I hope I shall make shift to go without him.

NERISSA If he should offer to choose, and choose the right casket, you should refuse to perform your father's will, if you should refuse to accept him.

PORTIA Therefore for fear of the worse, I pray thee set a deep glass of rhenish wine on the contrary casket, for if the devil be within, and that temptation without, I know he will choose it. I will do any thing Nerissa, ere I'll be married to a sponge.

NERISSA You need not fear, lady, the having any of these lords. They have acquainted me with their determinations, which is indeed to return to their home, and to trouble you with no more suit, unless you may be won by some other sort than your father's imposition, depending on the caskets.

PORTIA If I live to be as old as Sibylla, I will die as chaste as Diana, unless I be obtained by the manner of my father's will. I am glad this parcel of wooers are so reasonable, for there is not one among them but I dote on his very absence; and I pray God grant them a fair departure.

NERISSA Do you not remember lady, in your father's time, a Venetian, a scholar and a soldier, that came

Nerissa mentions a visitor from when Portia's father was alive. Portia remembers him favourably, and his name – Bassanio. As the suitors leave, another is about to arrive.

121 **forerunner** messenger

126 **condition** character

128 **shrive me** hear my confession

wive me become my husband

129 **Sirrah** (the ordinary form of address to inferiors) hither in company of the Marquis of Montferrat?

PORTIA Yes, yes, it was Bassanio, as I think, so was he called.

NERISSA True madam, he of all the men that ever my foolish eyes looked upon, was the best deserving a fair lady.

PORTIA I remember him well, and I remember him worthy of thy praise.

Enter a SERVING-MAN

How now, what news?

SERVING-MAN The four strangers seek for you madam to take their leave; and there is a forerunner come from a fifth, the Prince of Morocco, who brings word the prince his master will be here tonight.

PORTIA If I could bid the fifth welcome with so good a heart as I can bid the other four farewell, I should be glad of his approach. If he have the condition of a saint, and the complexion of a devil, I had rather he should shrive me than wive me. Come Nerissa. Sirrah go before. Whiles we shut the gates upon one wooer, another knocks at the door.

[*Exeunt*

Act 1 scenes 1 and 2

Who's who

In Act 1 scenes 1 and 2, we learn a good deal about the characters. For example, we learn what they are like, whether they are rich or poor, and how this affects their life. We can use a table like the one below to show what we learn about Antonio, Bassanio and Portia.
Copy the table out and fill in the missing information.

	Fact	**Scene / Lines**
Antonio	He is depressed without reason.	
		Scene 1: 9–14
	He is confident of his wealth.	
		Scene 1: 46–7
	He has a sad nature.	
Bassanio	He intends to visit a lady.	
		Scene 1: 130–1
		Scene 1: 146–8
	He has promised to tell Antonio how he can repay the debt.	
Portia		Scene 1: 161–2
		Scene 2: 1
	She has a problem with her father's will.	
	Nerissa tells her her father was right.	
		Scene 2: 107–10

Helping Antonio

Antonio's friends Salerio, Solanio, and Gratiano try to suggest what might be making him feel low. The speech ballons below sum up in modern English some of the things they say.

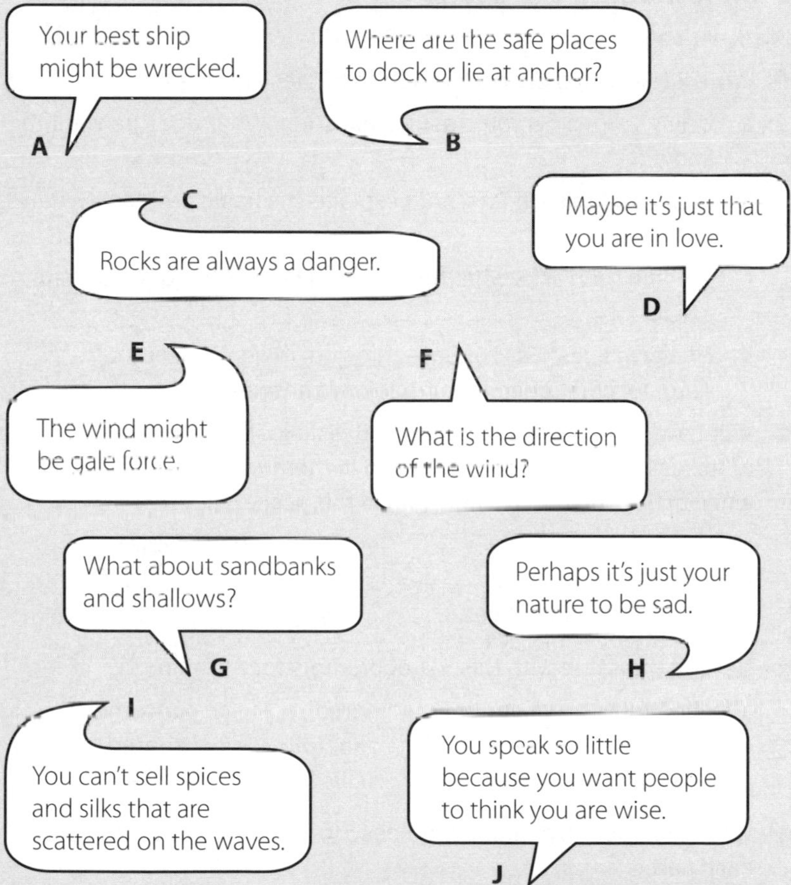

Work with a partner

1. Work out who said each of these things. Write down the letters A–J, and against each one write the name of the speaker.
2. In what order do their suggestions occur in scene 1? Write the letters in that order.

Performance: Antonio and Bassanio

Act 1 scene 1 ends with a conversation between Antonio and Bassanio that is central to the drama.

Understanding the scene

Work with a partner

1 Write a few words in answer to each of these questions:

   a In lines 119–21 Antonio asks a question. What does he want to know?

   b In his next speech Bassanio explains his basic problem. What is it?

   c Antonio then asks what he can do to help. What does Bassanio ask for?

   d Finally in lines 161–76, Bassanio gets to his answer to Antonio's first question. What is his answer?

2 What are your first impressions of Bassanio in this scene? Look at the list of prompts below. Which of them would you find useful when acting the part of Bassanio in this scene?

anxious	brash	embarrassed	feeble
grateful	greedy	proud	self-confident
selfish	talkative	tricksy	weak

3 Now do the same with this list of prompts for Antonio:

affectionate	anxious	bored	concerned
confused	embarrassed	generous	irritated
patient	puzzled	selfless	worried

4 Work together on a reading of lines 119–85. Decide who will play each part.

5 Each of you choose from the list of adjectives the ones you think describe best how your character should behave.

6 When you have read the scene together, discuss how it went and how it could be improved.

7 Now try it again.

So many suitors

In scene 2 Nerissa and Portia discuss the six suitors who have hoped to win her hand in marriage. Each has met her individually but none has tried the test of the caskets. Portia doesn't like any of them. What reasons does she give?

Work on your own

Make a table as follows and complete it, giving her reasons in your own words. The table has been started for you.

Suitor	Objections
The Neapolitan prince	All he can talk about is his horse and the fact that he can shoe it himself.
The County Palatine	
The French lord, Monsieur le Bon	
Falconbridge, the young English baron	
The Scottish lord	
The young German, the Duke of Saxony's nephew	

A modern version

Portia links each of these suitors to a particular country. But these young men could have come from any country.

Work with a partner

1 Imagine that you are writing a modern version of this scene. Think of two or three modern suitors, each with a personality that Portia would find just as irritating. (For example, one who boasts all the time about his car, or who hasn't got a sense of humour.)

2 For each one, write three or four sentences, describing him as Portia might have done.

Bassanio has approached Shylock for a loan to Antonio. Shylock considers Antonio's circumstances and credit rating.

1 **ducats** gold coins used in many European countries at this time; 3000 ducats was a lot of money. It would have been equal to a good year's income for a merchant like Antonio.

well yes, I see (he is considering the proposition)

6 **become bound** guarantee the amount, be liable if Bassanio cannot repay the loan

7 **May you stead me?** Can you help me?

pleasure satisfy

12 **good** i.e. 'good' for that amount of money and a 'good' person

13 **imputation** suggestion

16 **sufficient** able to guarantee the money

in supposition unsure

17 **an argosy** a merchant ship

18 **Rialto** This was the Exchange or business centre in medieval and renaissance Venice where merchants met to agree deals.

20 **squandered abroad** scattered recklessly around

24 **notwithstanding** nevertheless

25 **sufficient** capable of repaying such a sum

27 **Be assured** Do not doubt

Scene 3

Venice

Enter BASSANIO *and* SHYLOCK

SHYLOCK Three thousand ducats – well.

BASSANIO Ay sir, for three months.

SHYLOCK For three months – well.

BASSANIO For the which as I told you, Antonio shall be bound.

SHYLOCK Antonio shall become bound – well.

BASSANIO May you stead me? Will you pleasure me? Shall I know your answer?

SHYLOCK Three thousand ducats for three months, and Antonio bound.

BASSANIO Your answer to that.

SHYLOCK Antonio is a good man.

BASSANIO Have you heard any imputation to the contrary?

SHYLOCK Ho no, no, no, no. My meaning in saying he is a good man, is to have you understand me that he is sufficient – yet his means are in supposition: he hath an argosy bound to Tripolis, another to the Indies; I understand moreover upon the Rialto, he hath a third at Mexico, a fourth for England, and other ventures he hath squandered abroad. But ships are but boards, sailors but men; there be land-rats and water-rats, water-thieves and land-thieves, I mean pirates, and then there is the peril of waters, winds, and rocks. The man is notwithstanding sufficient. Three thousand ducats – I think I may take his bond.

BASSANIO Be assured you may.

Antonio arrives. We learn of Shylock's hatred for him. Shylock suggests that he may need to borrow in order to lend the money.

28 **be assured** obtain guarantees

29 **bethink me** consider the matter

31–2 **habitation ... into** When Jesus healed a man 'possessed by devils' he sent the devils into a herd of pigs which then rushed over a cliff into the sea. Jews traditionally do not eat pig-meat of any sort.

32 **Nazarite** inhabitant of Nazareth (i.e. Jesus Christ)

38 **fawning publican** cringing tax-gatherer ('Publicans' mentioned in the New Testament were Jews who gathered taxes from the Jewish population for their Roman rulers, and so were hated and despised.)

40 **low simplicity** simple folly

41 **gratis** free, without demanding interest

42 **usance** usury, the charging of interest on money loans

43 **catch ... hip** get a hold over him, get him at a disadvantage

44 **ancient grudge** i.e. the traditional hostility between Jews and Christians apparently originating in the accusation that the Jews were responsible for killing Jesus Christ

45 **rails** complains bitterly about

47 **thrift** profit

55 **furnish me** provide it for me

56 **signor** gentleman (form of address)

SHYLOCK I will be assured I may. And that I may be assured,
I will bethink me. May I speak with Antonio?

BASSANIO If it please you to dine with us.

SHYLOCK Yes, to smell pork, to eat of the habitation which your prophet the Nazarite conjured the devil into. I will buy with you, sell with you, talk with you, walk with you, and so following. But I will not eat with you, drink with you, nor pray with you. What news on the Rialto? Who is he comes here?

Enter ANTONIO

BASSANIO This is Signor Antonio.

SHYLOCK [*Aside*] How like a fawning publican he looks.
I hate him for he is a Christian.
But more, for that in low simplicity
He lends out money gratis, and brings down
The rate of usance here with us in Venice.
If I can catch him once upon the hip,
I will feed fat the ancient grudge I bear him.
He hates our sacred nation, and he rails
Even there where merchants most do congregate,
On me, my bargains, and my well-won thrift,
Which he calls interest. Cursed be my tribe
If I forgive him.

BASSANIO Shylock, do you hear?

SHYLOCK I am debating of my present store,
And by the near guess of my memory
I cannot instantly raise up the gross
Of full three thousand ducats. What of that?
Tubal a wealthy Hebrew of my tribe,
Will furnish me. But soft, how many months
Do you desire? [*To* ANTONIO] Rest you fair good signor,
Your worship was the last man in our mouths.

ANTONIO Shylock, albeit I neither lend nor borrow
By taking nor by giving of excess,

To justify shrewd dealing, Shylock tells the story of Jacob and Laban's sheep.

60 **ripe** immediate

61–2 **Is he ... would?** Does he know yet?

62 **would** would like, want

67 **Upon advantage** for interest

use it make a practice of it

68–87 **When Jacob ...** Shylock tells a story from the Old Testament (Genesis 30: 31–43) to justify using skill to take profit. Jacob had cheated his brother Esau and fled to his uncle Laban for fear that Esau would come and kill him. When he needed to leave Laban said he could take all the striped and spotted sheep. Jacob believed the old superstition that the unborn lambs would be affected by what the ewes saw during pregnancy. He peeled sticks to make patches of light and dark and set them up in front of the pregnant ewes. Later there were many patchily marked lambs for him to take away. (Today there is a breed of sheep with brown patches on their fleece. They are called Jacob sheep.)

75 **compromised** agreed

76 **eanlings** new-born lambs

77 **hire** wages

rank ready to breed

81 **pilled** peeled

83 **fulsome** pregnant

84 **eaning time** lambing

85 **Fall** drop

87 **thrift** sensible management of goods and money

88 **venture** undertaking

served for Jacob had worked for this outcome

89–90 **A thing ... heaven** it is made plain in the story that God intended this to happen

91 **Was ... good?** Is this story supposed to make the taking of interest good?

Yet to supply the ripe wants of my friend,
I'll break a custom. Is he yet possessed
How much ye would?

SHYLOCK Ay, ay, three thousand ducats.

ANTONIO And for three months.

SHYLOCK I had forgot – three months, you told me so.
Well then, your bond; and let me see – but hear you,
Methought you said you neither lend nor borrow
Upon advantage.

ANTONIO I do never use it.

SHYLOCK When Jacob grazed his uncle Laban's sheep –
This Jacob from our holy Abram was,
As his wise mother wrought in his behalf,
The third possessor; ay, he was the third –

ANTONIO And what of him? Did he take interest?

SHYLOCK No, not take interest, not as you would say
Directly interest; mark what Jacob did.
When Laban and himself were compromised
That all the eanlings which were streaked and pied
Should fall as Jacob's hire, the ewes being rank
In end of autumn turned to the rams,
And when the work of generation was
Between these woolly breeders in the act,
The skilful shepherd pilled me certain wands
And in the doing of the deed of kind
He stuck them up before the fulsome ewes,
Who then conceiving, did in eaning time
Fall parti-coloured lambs, and those were Jacob's.
This was a way to thrive, and he was blest;
And thrift is blessing if men steal it not.

ANTONIO This was a venture sir, that Jacob served for,
A thing not in his power to bring to pass,
But swayed and fashioned by the hand of heaven.
Was this inserted to make interest good?

Antonio mentions evil and 'a villain' almost in the same breath as he tries to clinch the loan. Shylock speaks of the way Antonio treats him.

95 **cite** quote

The devil ... purpose (a proverb derived from the Bible)

96 **An evil ... witness** A wicked man quoting from the Bible

99 **O ... hath** How wickedness can be made to look good

102 **beholding** under an obligation, indebted

104 **rated** reproved, scolded

105 **usances** Another word for the more usual 'usuries' – the taking of interest on a money loan.

106 **Still** Always

107 **sufferance** putting up with things, patience

109 **gabardine** An ankle-length loose coat, worn by men, especially Jews, in the Middle Ages.

112 **Go to** (an expression of amazement)

114 **did ... rheum** spat

115 **foot ... spurn** kick, push me aside with your foot

a stranger cur a dog that's not your own

116 **suit** request

120 **bondman's key** slave's voice

Or is your gold and silver ewes and rams?

SHYLOCK I cannot tell, I make it breed as fast.
But note me signor.

ANTONIO Mark you this Bassanio,
The devil can cite Scripture for his purpose.
An evil soul producing holy witness
Is like a villain with a smiling cheek,
A goodly apple rotten at the heart.
O what a goodly outside falsehood hath.

SHYLOCK Three thousand ducats – 'tis a good round sum.
Three months from twelve – then let me see, the rate –

ANTONIO Well Shylock, shall we be beholding to you?

SHYLOCK Signor Antonio, many a time and oft
In the Rialto you have rated me
About my moneys and my usances.
Still have I borne it with a patient shrug,
For sufferance is the badge of all our tribe.
You call me misbeliever, cut-throat dog,
And spit upon my Jewish gabardine,
And all for use of that which is mine own.
Well then, it now appears you need my help.
Go to then, you come to me, and you say,
'Shylock, we would have moneys' – you say so;
You that did void your rheum upon my beard,
And foot me as you spurn a stranger cur
Over your threshold – moneys is your suit.
What should I say to you? Should I not say,
'Hath a dog money? Is it possible
A cur can lend three thousand ducats?' Or
Shall I bend low, and in a bondman's key
With bated breath, and whispering humbleness
Say this:
'Fair sir, you spat on me on Wednesday last,
You spurned me such a day, another time
You called me dog; and for these courtesies

Shylock claims he does not want to prolong the quarrel but will lend without charging interest. He proposes the 'joke' forfeit of a pound of flesh. Antonio agrees, sure that his ships will come home in good time.

128 **spurn** strike

130–1 **for when ... friend** it is not in the nature of friendship to take interest on money lent to a friend

133 **break** fail to pay the money back on the agreed day

137–8 **take ... moneys** take not one penny of interest for my loan

137 **doit** a small Dutch coin; a worthless amount

139 **kind** natural generosity, kindness

141 **notary** solicitor

142 **single bond** bond with only one condition attached

merry sport merely as a joke

145–6 **let ... for** let us decide that the pledge shall be

152 **dwell in my necessity** remain in need

157 **Abram** A shortening of Abraham, the first of the great Hebrew leaders, revered by Jews, Christians, and Muslims.

158 **hard dealings** Shylock is claiming that because Christians are hard business people, they cannot see generosity when it is offered.

I'll lend you thus much moneys'?

ANTONIO I am as like to call thee so again,
To spit on thee again, to spurn thee too.
If thou wilt lend this money, lend it not
As to thy friends, for when did friendship take
A breed for barren metal of his friend?
But lend it rather to thine enemy,
Who if he break, thou mayst with better face
Exact the penalty.

SHYLOCK Why look you how you storm.
I would be friends with you, and have your love,
Forget the shames that you have stained me with,
Supply your present wants, and take no doit
Of usance for my moneys – and you'll not hear me.
This is kind I offer.

BASSANIO This were kindness.

SHYLOCK This kindness will I show –
Go with me to a notary, seal me there
Your single bond, and in a merry sport,
If you repay me not on such a day,
In such a place, such sum or sums as are
Expressed in the condition, let the forfeit
Be nominated for an equal pound
Of your fair flesh, to be cut off and taken
In what part of your body pleaseth me.

ANTONIO Content, i'faith, I'll seal to such a bond,
And say there is much kindness in the Jew.

BASSANIO You shall not seal to such a bond for me,
I'll rather dwell in my necessity.

ANTONIO Why fear not man, I will not forfeit it.
Within these two months, that's a month before
This bond expires, I do expect return
Of thrice three times the value of this bond.

SHYLOCK O father Abram, what these Christians are,
Whose own hard dealings teaches them suspect
The thoughts of others. Pray you tell me this,

Shylock insists there is no advantage for him in this strange bond. They arrange to meet at the solicitor's. Bassanio does not like the idea of this forfeit.

161 **exaction** demanding

163 **estimable** valuable, desirable

171 **purse the ducats** bag the money up

172 **see to** check up on

fearful timid

173 **unthrifty knave** careless, good-for-nothing servant

presently immediately

174 **Hie thee** Make haste

176 **I ... mind** Fair treatment coming from a villain worries me

If he should break his day, what should I gain
By the exaction of the forfeiture?
A pound of man's flesh taken from a man
Is not so estimable, profitable neither,
As flesh of muttons, beefs, or goats. I say,
To buy his favour, I extend this friendship.
If he will take it, so; if not, adieu,
And for my love I pray you wrong me not.

ANTONIO Yes Shylock, I will seal unto this bond.

SHYLOCK Then meet me forthwith at the notary's.
Give him direction for this merry bond,
And I will go and purse the ducats straight,
See to my house, left in the fearful guard
Of an unthrifty knave; and presently
I will be with you.

ANTONIO Hie thee gentle Jew.

[*Exit* SHYLOCK

The Hebrew will turn Christian, he grows kind.

BASSANIO I like not fair terms and a villain's mind.

ANTONIO Come on, in this there can be no dismay,
My ships come home a month before the day.

[*Exeunt*

The Prince of Morocco arrives to choose between the caskets. He speaks proudly of his colour, but fears it may bother Portia. She reassures him.

SD ***Flourish Cornets*** Fanfare of trumpets

SD ***tawny*** light brown

SD ***train*** attendants

1 **Mislike ... complexion** Do not dislike me for my colour

2 **shadowed livery** dark uniform (the colour of his skin)
burnished brightly shining

3 **near bred** closely related

5 **Phoebus** the sun god in Greek mythology

6 **make incision** make a cut in our skin

8 **aspect** appearance

9 **Hath ... valiant** made the bravest men afraid

10 **The ... clime** the most favoured young women of our region

12 **steal your thoughts** unless it would win you over to me

14 **By nice ... eyes** by a fussy insistence on appearances alone

15 **the lottery ... destiny** the fact that my fate is to be decided by chance

17–18 **scanted ... wit** restricted me by both his will and wisdom; Portia is claiming that his colour does not matter to her. If her father had not set up the three caskets method of choosing her husband for her, then the Prince of Morocco would still have stood an equal chance with any of the suitors she has seen so far.

Act Two

Scene 1

Belmont

Flourish Cornets. Enter the PRINCE OF MOROCCO *(a tawny Moor all in white) and three or four followers accordingly; with* PORTIA, NERISSA, *and their train*

MOROCCO Mislike me not for my complexion,
The shadowed livery of the burnished sun,
To whom I am a neighbour, and near bred.
Bring me the fairest creature northward born,
Where Phoebus' fire scarce thaws the icicles,
And let us make incision for your love,
To prove whose blood is reddest, his or mine.
I tell thee lady, this aspect of mine
Hath feared the valiant. By my love I swear
The best-regarded virgins of our clime
Have loved it too. I would not change this hue,
Except to steal your thoughts, my gentle queen.

PORTIA In terms of choice I am not solely led
By nice direction of a maiden's eyes;
Besides, the lottery of my destiny
Bars me the right of voluntary choosing.
But if my father had not scanted me,
And hedged me by his wit to yield myself
His wife who wins me by that means I told you,
Yourself, renowned Prince, then stood as fair
As any comer I have looked on yet
For my affection.

MOROCCO Even for that I thank you.
Therefore I pray you lead me to the caskets

The Prince gives some account of his bravery but recognises it can count for nothing when it is chance which will decide.

24 **scimitar** a short curved sword, single-edged

25 **Sophy** the Shah of Persia

26 **Sultan Solyman** Suleiman the Magnificent (leader of the Turkish Empire from 1520 to 1566)

27 **o'erstare** outstare

28 **Outbrave** be braver than

31–7 **But, alas ... attain** He realises that however bold and brave and experienced he is, this will all count for nothing. It is chance that must decide his fate.

32 **Hercules** the Greek hero (a well-known example of bravery and strength)

Lichas Hercules' servant and companion, who handed him a shirt to wear, not knowing it had been poisoned.

35 **Alcides** the original name of Hercules (The agonising poison threw him into a rage.)

To try my fortune. By this scimitar
That slew the Sophy, and a Persian prince
That won three fields of Sultan Solyman,
I would o'erstare the sternest eyes that look,
Outbrave the heart most daring on the earth,
Pluck the young sucking cubs from the she-bear,
Yea, mock the lion when he roars for prey,
To win thee lady. But, alas the while,
If Hercules and Lichas play at dice
Which is the better man, the greater throw
May turn by fortune from the weaker hand:
So is Alcides beaten by his rage,
And so may I, blind Fortune leading me,
Miss that which one unworthier may attain,
And die with grieving.

PORTIA You must take your chance,
And either not attempt to choose at all,
Or swear before you choose, if you choose wrong
Never to speak to lady afterward
In way of marriage. Therefore be advised.

MOROCCO Nor will not. Come bring me unto my chance.

PORTIA First forward to the temple, after dinner
Your hazard shall be made.

MOROCCO Good fortune then,
To make me blest or cursed'st among men.

[*Cornets. Exeunt*

Act 1 scene 3 and Act 2 scene 1

Character: Shylock

In Act 1 scene 3 we meet Shylock doing business as a professional money-lender. He has to work out whether the deal with Antonio will be satisfactory for him. But he also expresses his hurt and his dislike of this borrower.

Work with a partner

1 Put the following statements of Shylock's in the order in which he says them:

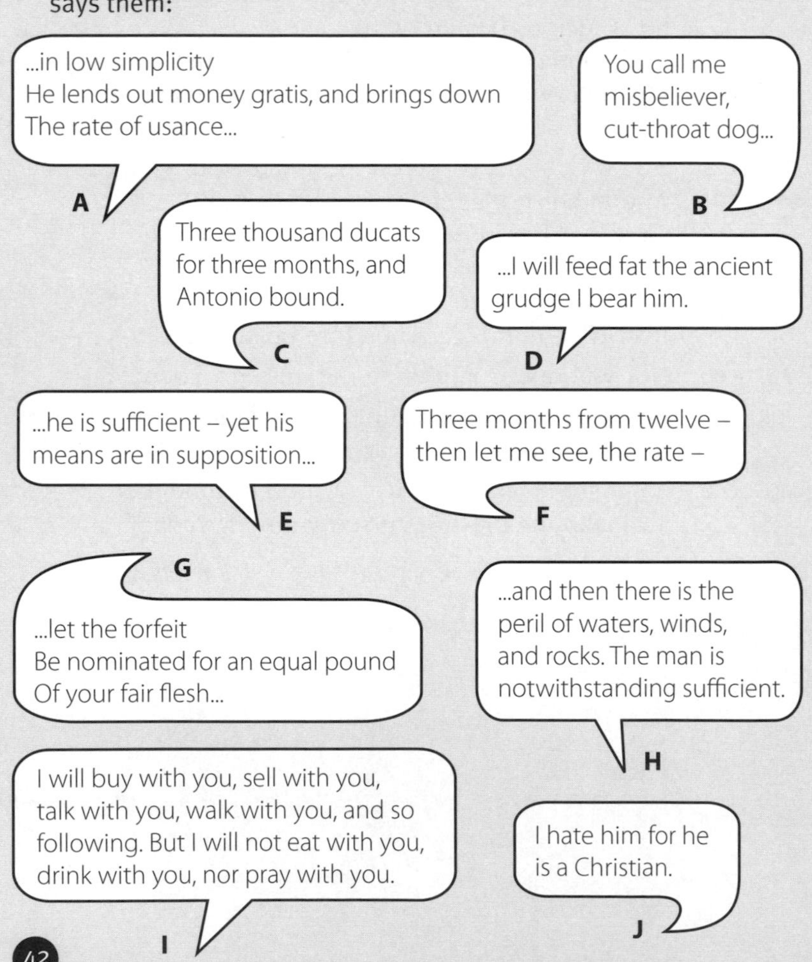

2 Now put the statements into two groups:

  a Statements that are professional – purely about Shylock's business interests

  b Statements that are personal, racial, or emotional.

Performance

Act 1 scene 3 lines 1–13

In the opening to this scene, it is difficult at first to work out what is going through Shylock's mind. The lines can be performed in different ways.

Work with a partner

1 Cast the parts.

2 Read the lines aloud.

3 Now each choose one of the prompts below to help you interpret the lines.

Shylock	Bassanio
He is very suspicious of this deal – he thinks it may be a trick.	He hates having to talk to Shylock like this. The sooner it is over, the better.
He is just playing Bassanio along, to show his power.	He is very anxious; it doesn't look as if Shylock is going to agree.
He wants the deal, but he wants to hide his interest by pretending not to be interested.	He has explained this to Shylock three times already and is beginning to lose patience.

4 Act the lines following your chosen prompt.

5 Now each choose a different prompt and perform the lines again.

6 Discuss the two versions: which do you think was better, and why?

Extension

Repeat the exercise with lines 35–56, this time making up your own prompts.

Issues: Who's right? Who's wrong?

In Act 1 scene 3, Shylock expresses his thoughts and feelings about the way he thinks Antonio and his friends have treated him. He has clearly been very badly treated. But is all the right on one side?

Work on your own

1 Read through the scene again.

2 Use a table like the one below to collect your ideas about this. It has been started for you.

For Shylock	Point	Supporting quotation	Comments
	Antonio criticises Shylock in public.	...he rails | Even there where merchants most do congregate, | On me... (lines 45–7)	Antonio takes pleasure in humiliating Shylock in front of his fellow merchants.

Against Shylock	Point	Supporting quotation	Comments
	Shylock hates Christians as much as Antonio hates Jews.	I hate him for he is a Christian. (line 39)	Just the fact that Antonio is a Christian is enough for Shylock to hate him.

Work in a group of three or four

3 Share your ideas and prepare a table like the one above that contains all your group's ideas.

4 Present your ideas to the rest of the class.

Production: Act 2 scene 1

Earlier in the play Portia described six suitors. They came hoping to marry a rich woman. Now we meet the next suitor. The Prince of Morocco has much more status: a country of his own, courtiers and servants.

Work on your own

1 Read the scene through again.

Work in a group of three or four

2 Discuss how you could stage this scene. Think about these points:
   - a How many characters are on stage during the scene?
   - b What impression do the stage directions at the beginning of the scene give you?
   - c What kind of setting/scenery will you need?
   - d What about lighting?
   - e What will the costumes be like? (Think about colours, materials, and styles.)
   - f Will there be music? (If so, what kind, and when?)
   - g There are three long speeches in the scene. How should these be staged? What do the other characters do during them?

3 Decide who will be responsible for:
   - a designing the setting
   - b designing the costumes
   - c planning the lighting and music.

4 Make notes and/or drawings to show your ideas.

5 Share them with the group and discuss improvements.

6 Present your ideas to the rest of the class.

Launcelot Gobbo is having a battle with his conscience about whether to leave Shylock's service. He wants to go, but his sense of duty is telling him to stay.

1 **will serve me** must allow me

2 **fiend** devil

7–8 **as aforesaid** as mentioned earlier

10 **pack** go off

Fia! Forward!

13 **hanging … neck** holding back; his conscience is trying to stop his heart taking action.

17 **something** somewhat, rather

smack 1) have a trace of 2) kiss noisily

grow to lean towards

21 **counsel** advise

23 **God … mark** The 'mark' was possibly a reference to the cross and this remark was supposed to protect the speaker after a mention of the devil.

25 **saving your reverence** Of similar force to the previous remark, a polite apology.

27 **incarnation** Launcelot's mistake for 'incarnate' – in bodily form.

Scene 2

Venice

Enter LAUNCELOT

LAUNCELOT Certainly my conscience will serve me to run from this Jew my master. The fiend is at mine elbow, and tempts me, saying to me, 'Gobbo, Launcelot Gobbo, good Launcelot', or 'Good Gobbo', or 'Good Launcelot Gobbo, use your legs, take the start, run away'. My conscience says, 'No, take heed honest Launcelot, take heed honest Gobbo', or as aforesaid, 'Honest Launcelot Gobbo; do not run, scorn running with thy heels'. Well, the most courageous fiend bids me pack: 'Fia!' says the fiend; 'Away!' says the fiend; 'For the heavens, rouse up a brave mind', says the fiend, 'and run.' Well, my conscience, hanging about the neck of my heart, says very wisely to me: 'My honest friend Launcelot, being an honest man's son', or rather an honest woman's son – for indeed my father did something smack, something grow to, he had a kind of taste – well, my conscience says, 'Launcelot budge not.' 'Budge,' says the fiend. 'Budge not', says my conscience. 'Conscience', say I, 'you counsel well.' 'Fiend', say I, 'you counsel well.' To be ruled by my conscience, I should stay with the Jew my master, who – God bless the mark – is a kind of devil; and to run away from the Jew I should be ruled by the fiend, who – saving your reverence – is the devil himself. Certainly the Jew is the very devil incarnation, and in my conscience, my conscience is but a kind of hard conscience, to offer to counsel me to stay with the Jew. The fiend gives the more friendly counsel. I will run, fiend; my heels are at your command, I will run.

Launcelot's father is looking for Shylock's house, to find his son. Launcelot deliberately confuses the old man and then tells him his son is dead.

34 **true-begotten** real, true

35 **sand-blind** half blind

high-gravel blind almost completely blind (He is making these terms up.)

36 **confusions** He means 'conclusions'.

40 **marry** indeed

41 **of no hand** straight on

43 **By God's sonties** An oath invented by old Gobbo; 'sonties' may be 'saints'.

46 **Master Launcelot** Launcelot still tries to confuse the old man by using a form of address meant for masters, not servants.

51 **well to live** well off (contradicting 'exceeding poor man')

52 **'a** he

54 **Your worship's friend** He uses another polite form to avoid 'master'.

55 **ergo** Latin word meaning 'therefore'. In his comic characters Shakespeare makes fun of its overuse.

57 **an't** if it

61 **the Sisters Three** A reference to the Fates in Greek mythology, three old women. One spins thread of a person's life, the second measures it and the third cuts it off (when they die).

62 **deceased** Launcelot, to confuse, pretends Gobbo's son is dead.

Enter OLD GOBBO *with a basket*

GOBBO Master young man, you I pray you, which is the way to Master Jew's?

LAUNCELOT [*Aside*] O heavens, this is my true-begotten father, who being more than sand-blind, high-gravel blind, knows me not – I will try confusions with him.

GOBBO Master young gentleman, I pray you which is the way to Master Jew's?

LAUNCELOT Turn up on your right hand at the next turning, but at the next turning of all on your left; marry at the very next turning turn of no hand, but turn down indirectly to the Jew's house.

GOBBO By God's sonties 'twill be a hard way to hit. Can you tell me whether one Launcelot that dwells with him, dwell with him or no?

LAUNCELOT Talk you of young Master Launcelot? [*Aside*] Mark me now, now will I raise the waters. Talk you of young Master Launcelot?

GOBBO No master sir, but a poor man's son. His father, though I say it, is an honest exceeding poor man, and God be thanked, well to live.

LAUNCELOT Well, let his father be what 'a will, we talk of young Master Launcelot.

GOBBO Your worship's friend and Launcelot sir.

LAUNCELOT But I pray you, ergo old man, ergo I beseech you, talk you of young Master Launcelot?

GOBBO Of Launcelot an't please your mastership.

LAUNCELOT Ergo Master Launcelot. Talk not of Master Launcelot father; for the young gentleman – according to Fates and Destinies and such odd sayings, the Sisters Three and such branches of learning – is indeed deceased, or, as you would say in plain terms, gone to heaven.

GOBBO Marry God forbid, the boy was the very staff of my

Launcelot now takes pity on his father and admits he is his son. The old man takes some convincing.

66 **cudgel** stick, club

hovel-post one of the upright stakes which help to form a poor shack

74–5 **it is ... child** The **proverb** is really 'It is a wise child that knows its own father'.

86 **man** servant

90 **Lord ... be** May God be praised

91–2 **thou hast ... tail** Old Gobbo has his hands on Launcelot's head, not on his chin.

92 **fill-horse** cart-horse

age, my very prop.

LAUNCELOT Do I look like a cudgel, or a hovel-post, a staff, or a prop? Do you know me father?

GOBBO Alack the day, I know you not young gentleman, but I pray you tell me, is my boy – God rest his soul – alive or dead?

LAUNCELOT Do you not know me father?

GOBBO Alack sir I am sand-blind, I know you not.

LAUNCELOT Nay indeed, if you had your eyes, you might fail of the knowing me: it is a wise father that knows his own child. [*Kneels*] Well, old man, I will tell you news of your son – give me your blessing – truth will come to light. Murder cannot be hid long, a man's son may, but at the length truth will out.

GOBBO Pray you, sir, stand up. I am sure you are not Launcelot, my boy.

LAUNCELOT Pray you, let's have no more fooling about it, but give me your blessing. I am Launcelot your boy that was, your son that is, your child that shall be.

GOBBO I cannot think you are my son.

LAUNCELOT I know not what I shall think of that; but I am Launcelot the Jew's man, and I am sure Margery your wife is my mother.

GOBBO Her name is Margery indeed. I'll be sworn if thou be Launcelot, thou art mine own flesh and blood. Lord worshipped might he be, what a beard hast thou got; thou hast got more hair on thy chin than Dobbin my fill-horse has on his tail.

LAUNCELOT It should seem then that Dobbin's tail grows backward. I am sure he had more hair of this tail than I have of my face when I last saw him.

GOBBO Lord how art thou changed. How dost thou and thy master agree? I have brought him a present. How 'gree you now?

Launcelot admits he has decided to seek a new master. Bassanio is his choice and, when he enters, both father and son put Launcelot's case.

99–100 **set ... away** staked everything on running away

101 **some ground** quite a distance

very thorough, complete, true

102 **halter** noose

103–4 **you may ... ribs** Launcelot, claiming he has become thin in the Jew's service, gets 'finger' and 'ribs' the wrong way round. He often confuses words and here the comic effect could be emphasised on stage by Launcelot spreading his fingers down his ribs and getting his blind father to feel how bony they are.

106 **rare** splendid

liveries servants' uniforms

106–7 **as ... ground** to the ends of the earth

108 **I am a Jew** I shall turn into a villain

110 **let ... hasted** speed things up

112 **put ... making** get the uniforms made

113 **anon** shortly

116 **Gramercy** God bless your worship

aught anything

120 **infection** Gobbo means 'affection'.

125 **scarce cater cousins** hardly good friends

128 **frutify** He means 'notify'.

LAUNCELOT Well, well, but for mine own part, as I have set up my rest to run away, so I will not rest till I have run some ground. My master's a very Jew. Give him a present? Give him a halter. I am famished in his service; you may tell every finger I have with my ribs. Father, I am glad you are come, give me your present to one Master Bassanio, who indeed gives rare new liveries. If I serve not him, I will run as far as God has any ground. O rare fortune, here comes the man. To him father, for I am a Jew if I serve the Jew any longer.

Enter BASSANIO, *with* LEONARDO *and a follower or two*

BASSANIO You may do so, but let it be so hasted that supper be ready at the farthest by five of the clock. See these letters delivered, put the liveries to making, and desire Gratiano to come anon to my lodging.

[*Exit a Servant*

LAUNCELOT To him father.

GOBBO God bless your worship.

BASSANIO Gramercy, wouldst thou aught with me?

GOBBO Here's my son sir, a poor boy –

LAUNCELOT Not a poor boy sir, but the rich Jew's man that would sir – as my father shall specify –

GOBBO He hath a great infection sir, as one would say, to serve –

LAUNCELOT Indeed the short and the long is, I serve the Jew, and have a desire – as my father shall specify –

GOBBO His master and he – saving your worship's reverence – are scarce cater cousins –

LAUNCELOT To be brief, the very truth is that the Jew, having done me wrong, doth cause me – as my father, being I hope an old man, shall frutify unto you –

Bassanio takes Launcelot on as his servant. Launcelot, with his father, goes to take his leave of Shylock.

130 **suit** request

131 **impertinent** He means 'pertinent' – relevant.

137 **defect** He means 'effect'.

140 **preferred** recommended

preferment promotion

143 **parted** shared

147–8 **inquire ... out** find my house

149 **more guarded** with more trimming

150 **I ... service** I can't get a job (He is being sarcastic.)

151–3 **Well ... fortune** The reference here is to palmistry – the reading of palms for fortune-telling. The 'table' is the rectangle formed by the four main lines on the palm of the hand. Launcelot considers his reading means he will have many wives.

156 **coming-in** income

157–60 **to 'scape ... gear** Launcelot's reading of his palm continues to show him a satisfactory future – a long enough life and plenty of sex.

157 **'scape** escape

160 **gear** business

161 **twinkling** in the twinkling of an eye

GOBBO I have here a dish of doves that would bestow upon your worship, and my suit is –

LAUNCELOT In very brief, the suit is impertinent to myself, as your worship shall know by this honest old man, and though I say it, though old man, yet poor man, my father.

BASSANIO One speak for both. What would you?

LAUNCELOT Serve you sir.

GOBBO That is the very defect of the matter sir.

BASSANIO I know thee well, thou hast obtained thy suit.
Shylock thy master spoke with me this day,
And hath preferred thee, if it be preferment
To leave a rich Jew's service, to become
The follower of so poor a gentleman.

LAUNCELOT The old proverb is very well parted between my master Shylock and you sir: you have the grace of God sir, and he hath enough.

BASSANIO Thou speak'st it well. Go father with thy son.
Take leave of thy old master, and inquire
My lodging out. Give him a livery
More guarded than his fellows'. See it done.

LAUNCELOT Father in. I cannot get a service, no, I have ne'er a tongue in my head. Well, if any man in Italy have a fairer table which doth offer to swear upon a book, I shall have good fortune. Go to, here's a simple line of life, here's a small trifle of wives. Alas, fifteen wives is nothing, eleven widows and nine maids is a simple coming-in for one man; and then to 'scape drowning thrice, and to be in peril of my life with the edge of a feather-bed, here are simple scapes. Well, if Fortune be a woman, she's a good wench for this gear. Father come; I'll take my leave of the Jew in the twinkling.

[*Exeunt* LAUNCELOT *and* OLD GOBBO

BASSANIO I pray thee, good Leonardo, think on this.

Gratiano wants to accompany Bassanio to Belmont. Bassanio is not keen as he finds Gratiano rather loud and rough, and his future may depend on the impression he makes on Portia. Gratiano promises to behave.

163 **orderly bestowed** neatly put away

164–5 **I do ... acquaintance** I am offering a feast tonight to my best friends

166 **endeavours** efforts

167 **Yonder** Over there

173 **rude** uncivilised, rough

174 **Parts** qualities

become suit

177 **liberal** freely

178 **allay** repress, subdue

179 **skipping spirit** thoughtless behaviour

180 **misconstrued** misinterpreted, misunderstood

181 **lose my hopes** ruin my plans

182 **habit** appearance, behaviour

184 **demurely** seriously

185 **grace** A short prayer before a meal asking God's blessing on the food and those about to eat.

hood cover

187 **Use ... civility** follow the rules of good manners

188–9 **well ... grandam** with considerable practice in appearing grave to please his grandmother

190 **we ... bearing** I shall keep an eye on your behaviour

These things being bought and orderly bestowed,
Return in haste, for I do feast tonight
My best-esteemed acquaintance; hie thee, go.

LEONARDO My best endeavours shall be done herein.

Enter GRATIANO

GRATIANO Where is your master?

LEONARDO Yonder sir, he walks.

[*Exit*

GRATIANO Signor Bassanio.

BASSANIO Gratiano.

GRATIANO I have a suit to you.

BASSANIO You have obtained it.

GRATIANO You must not deny me, I must go with you to Belmont.

BASSANIO Why then you must. But hear thee Gratiano,
Thou art too wild, too rude and bold of voice,
Parts that become thee happily enough,
And in such eyes as ours appear not faults,
But where thou art not known, why there they show
Something too liberal. Pray thee take pain
To allay with some cold drops of modesty
Thy skipping spirit, lest through thy wild behaviour
I be misconstrued in the place I go to,
And lose my hopes.

GRATIANO Signor Bassanio, hear me:
If I do not put on a sober habit,
Talk with respect, and swear but now and then,
Wear prayer-books in my pocket, look demurely,
Nay more, while grace is saying hood mine eyes
Thus with my hat, and sigh and say, 'amen';
Use all the observance of civility
Like one well studied in a sad ostent
To please his grandam, never trust me more.

BASSANIO Well, we shall see your bearing.

Bassanio parts from Gratiano, who promises to join his party that evening with Lorenzo.

191 **I bar tonight** I'm not counting tonight

gauge judge

192 **were** would be a

193–4 **I would ... mirth** I would prefer you to be the life and soul of the party

195 **purpose merriment** intend to have a good time

At Shylock's house, Launcelot is saying goodbye to Jessica. She hands him a letter for Lorenzo. They are planning to get married. She will convert to Christianity.

10 **exhibit** He probably means 'inhibit' – prevent his tongue from saying what he felt.

11 **pagan** heathen (it also meant 'prostitute')

11–12 **play the knave** go in for trickery

13 **these foolish drops** his tears

16 **heinous** hateful, infamous

19 **manners** morals

GRATIANO Nay but I bar tonight, you shall not gauge me
By what we do tonight.

BASSANIO No that were pity.
I would entreat you rather to put on
Your boldest suit of mirth, for we have friends
That purpose merriment. But fare you well,
I have some business.

GRATIANO And I must to Lorenzo and the rest.
But we will visit you at supper-time.

[*Exeunt*

Scene 3

Venice

Enter JESSICA *and* LAUNCELOT

JESSICA I am sorry thou wilt leave my father so:
Our house is hell, and thou, a merry devil,
Didst rob it of some taste of tediousness.
But fare thee well, there is a ducat for thee;
And Launcelot, soon at supper shalt thou see
Lorenzo, who is thy new master's guest.
Give him this letter, do it secretly,
And so farewell: I would not have my father
See me in talk with thee.

LAUNCELOT Adieu, tears exhibit my tongue. Most beautiful pagan, most sweet Jew, if a Christian do not play the knave and get thee, I am much deceived. But adieu: these foolish drops do something drown my manly spirit. Adieu. [*Exit* LAUNCELOT

JESSICA Farewell good Launcelot.
Alack, what heinous sin is it in me
To be ashamed to be my father's child.
But though I am a daughter to his blood,
I am not to his manners. O Lorenzo
If thou keep promise, I shall end this strife,
Become a Christian and thy loving wife. [*Exit*

Lorenzo and friends are planning their arrangements for the masque that evening. Launcelot gives Lorenzo the letter from Jessica and he sends a message in return.

2 **Disguise ... lodging** change our clothes at home and put on masks

5 **torch-bearers** people who carried torches to light the way

6 **vile** horrible

quaintly cleverly, ingeniously

7 **undertook** undertaken, done

9 **furnish us** provide ourselves with what we need

10 **break up this** open the letter by breaking the seal

11 **seem to signify** give you the news

12 **fair hand** attractive handwriting

14 **fair hand** beautiful hand

24 **Ay marry** Yes indeed

straight straight away, immediately

Scene 4

Venice

Enter GRATIANO, LORENZO, SALERIO, *and* SOLANIO

LORENZO Nay, we will slink away in supper-time,
Disguise us at my lodging and return,
All in an hour.

GRATIANO We have not made good preparation.

SALERIO We have not spoke us yet of torch-bearers.

SOLANIO 'Tis vile unless it may be quaintly ordered,
And better in my mind not undertook.

LORENZO 'Tis now but four o'clock, we have two hours
To furnish us.

Enter LAUNCELOT *with a letter*

Friend Launcelot what's the news?

LAUNCELOT An it shall please you to break up this, it shall seem to signify.

LORENZO I know the hand. In faith 'tis a fair hand,
And whiter than the paper it writ on
Is the fair hand that writ.

GRATIANO Love-news in faith.

LAUNCELOT By your leave sir.

LORENZO Whither goest thou?

LAUNCELOT Marry sir to bid my old master the Jew to sup tonight with my new master the Christian.

LORENZO Hold here, take this. Tell gentle Jessica
I will not fail her; speak it privately.

[*Exit* LAUNCELOT

Go gentlemen,
Will you prepare you for this masque tonight?
I am provided of a torch-bearer.

SALERIO Ay marry, I'll be gone about it straight.

Lorenzo tells Gratiano of Jessica's arrangements to provide herself with a disguise and with money.

29 **must needs** have to

31 **furnished** provided

32 **page's suit** Jessica intends to elope dressed as a page boy, their torch-bearer for the masque.

34 **gentle** noble, with a possible **play on words** (see Glossary p. 242), i.e. 'gentile' – since Jessica is to marry a Christian.

35 **cross her foot** cross her path

35–7 **never ... Jew** may she never suffer bad luck unless it comes from her being the daughter of a heathen Jew

36 **Unless she do it** The word 'she' in this line refers to 'misfortune' in the previous line. This is an example of **personification**, see Glossary p. 242.

37 **issue** child

faithless unbelieving

38 **peruse this** read this through

Shylock and Launcelot take leave of one another.

3 **gormandise** eat greedily

5 **rend apparel out** let your clothes get torn

7 **Who ... call?** Who is telling you to call?

8 **was ... me** used to tell me all the time

SOLANIO And so will I.

LORENZO Meet me and Gratiano
At Gratiano's lodging some hour hence.

SALERIO 'Tis good we do so.

[*Exeunt* SALERIO *and* SOLANIO

GRATIANO Was not that letter from fair Jessica?

LORENZO I must needs tell thee all. She hath directed
How I shall take her from her father's house,
What gold and jewels she is furnished with,
What page's suit she hath in readiness.
If e'er the Jew her father come to heaven,
It will be for his gentle daughter's sake.
And never dare misfortune cross her foot,
Unless she do it under this excuse,
That she is issue to a faithless Jew.
Come go with me, peruse this as thou goest
Fair Jessica shall be my torch-bearer.

[*Exeunt*

Scene 5

Venice

Enter SHYLOCK *and* LAUNCELOT

SHYLOCK Well, thou shalt see, thy eyes shall be thy judge,
The difference of old Shylock and Bassanio –
What Jessica! – thou shalt not gormandise
As thou hast done with me – What Jessica!
And sleep, and snore, and rend apparel out –
Why Jessica, I say!

LAUNCELOT Why Jessica!

SHYLOCK Who bids thee call? I do not bid thee call.

LAUNCELOT Your worship was wont to tell me I could do nothing without bidding.

Enter JESSICA

JESSICA Call you? What is your will?

Shylock does not want to dine with Bassanio – he is even more reluctant when he hears about the masque. Jessica is instructed to shut up the house and stay indoors. Launcelot delivers Lorenzo's message to her.

12 **wherefore** why

13 **bid for** invited out of

15 **prodigal** lavish, wasteful

17 **ill a-brewing towards** trouble brewing to disturb

rest peace of mind

18 **For ... tonight** A dream about money was supposed to mean bad luck.

20 **reproach** Launcelot means 'approach', but in line 21 Shylock picks up what he actually says.

23 **masque** Usually a masque was a play or performance with music and dancing in a private house.

24–5 **Black Monday** Easter Monday; Launcelot gives a nonsensical horoscope to fit in with Shylock's dreams and fears.

30 **wry-necked fife** flute-player with twisted neck (as often happens while playing the flute)

31 **Clamber ... casements** do not climb up to the windows

33 **varnished** painted, or masked

35 **shallow foppery** foolish larking about

38 **sirrah** A form of address to a servant.

44 **Hagar's offspring** Ishmael, Abraham's son by Hagar, an Egyptian slave, was a gentile and an outcast.

46 **patch** fool

47 **profit** benefit, usefulness

SHYLOCK I am bid forth to supper Jessica;
There are my keys. But wherefore should I go?
I am not bid for love, they flatter me.
But yet I'll go in hate, to feed upon
The prodigal Christian. Jessica my girl,
Look to my house. I am right loath to go,
There is some ill a-brewing towards my rest,
For I did dream of money bags tonight.

LAUNCELOT I beseech you sir, go. My young master doth expect your reproach.

SHYLOCK So do I his.

LAUNCELOT And they have conspired together – I will not say you shall see a masque, but if you do, then it was not for nothing that my nose fell a-bleeding on Black Monday last, at six o'clock i' the morning, falling out that year on Ash-Wednesday was four year in th'afternoon.

SHYLOCK What, are there masques? Hear you me Jessica:
Lock up my doors, and when you hear the drum
And the vile squealing of the wry-necked fife,
Clamber not you up to the casements then,
Nor thrust your head into the public street
To gaze on Christian fools with varnished faces.
But stop my house's ears, I mean my casements,
Let not the sound of shallow foppery enter
My sober house. By Jacob's staff, I swear
I have no mind of feasting forth tonight.
But I will go. Go you before me sirrah,
Say I will come.

LAUNCELOT I will go before, sir. Mistress, look out at window for all this –
There will come a Christian by
Will be worth a Jewes' eye. [*Exit*

SHYLOCK What says that fool of Hagar's offspring, ha?

JESSICA His words were, 'Farewell, mistress', nothing else.

SHYLOCK The patch is kind enough, but a huge feeder,
Snail-slow in profit, and he sleeps by day

Shylock goes off to dine with Bassanio, unaware that Jessica is about to elope with a Christian.

48 **wildcat** a nocturnal animal (and so sleeps by day)

Drones male honey-bees, non-workers

54 **Fast ... find** what is firmly shut up will stay secure

Lorenzo's friends are waiting for him. He is late.

1 **penthouse** overhanging upper storey of a house (in Elizabethan England, not in Venice)

2 **make stand** wait

3 **it is marvel** it is amazing

he ... hour he is late

5–7 **O ... unforfeited** the doves of Venus (Roman goddess of love) fly much faster to a couple who have just fallen in love than to those in a long engagement

8 **holds** holds true

10–12 **untread ... first** paces home again with the untired energy with which he first stepped out

14 **younger** younger son

prodigal spendthrift (younger son) of the parable in the Bible (Luke 15: 11–32)

15 **scarfed bark** ship decorated with flags and pennants

16 **strumpet** prostitute (who will embrace anyone and is faithful to no one)

18 **over-weathered** weather-beaten

ribs 1) the ship's timbers 2) the skinny son's ribs

19 **rent** torn

More than the wildcat. Drones hive not with me,
Therefore I part with him, and part with him
To one that I would have him help to waste
His borrowed purse. Well Jessica, go in –
Perhaps I will return immediately –
Do as I bid you, shut doors after you.
Fast bind, fast find,
A proverb never stale in thrifty mind. *[Exit*

JESSICA Farewell, and if my fortune be not crossed,
I have a father, you a daughter lost.

[Exit

Scene 6

Venice

Enter the masquers GRATIANO *and* SALERIO

GRATIANO This is the penthouse under which Lorenzo
Desired us to make stand.

SALERIO His hour is almost past.

GRATIANO And it is marvel he out-dwells his hour,
For lovers ever run before the clock.

SALERIO O ten times faster Venus' pigeons fly
To seal love's bonds new-made, than they are wont
To keep obliged faith unforfeited.

GRATIANO That ever holds: who riseth from a feast
With that keen appetite that he sits down?
Where is the horse that doth untread again
His tedious measures with the unbated fire
That he did pace them first? All things that are,
Are with more spirit chased than enjoyed.
How like a younger or a prodigal
The scarfed bark puts from her native bay,
Hugged and embraced by the strumpet wind.
How like the prodigal doth she return,
With over-weathered ribs and ragged sails,
Lean, rent, and beggared by the strumpet wind.

Lorenzo arrives, and soon after, Jessica appears. She is dressed as a boy, and throws down a casket containing money she has taken from Shylock. She is alarmed at having to appear in public, dressed this way.

21 **abode** delay

23 **play ... wives** the opposite but similar action to what Jessica is doing

27 **Albeit** even though

33 **pains** trouble

35 **exchange** She has changed into boy's clothing to elope, she has exchanged Shylock for Lorenzo, and she has turned into a thief – all for love.

37 **pretty** ingenious

41 **hold ... shames** shine a light on what I'm ashamed of

42 **light** well-lit, obvious, and a **play on words** (see Glossary p. 242). Light also meant immoral.

43 **office of discovery** revealing work (The job of a torch-bearer, hired for the evening, was to light his master through the dark and dirty streets.)

45 **garnish** outfit

47 **close** secretive (Lorenzo says that night, which is hiding her away, is itself running out.)

48 **we are stayed for** they are expecting us

49 **gild** supply

SALERIO Here comes Lorenzo, more of this hereafter.

Enter LORENZO

LORENZO Sweet friends, your patience for my long abode.
Not I, but my affairs, have made you wait.
When you shall please to play the thieves for wives
I'll watch as long for you then. Approach.
Here dwells my father Jew. Ho, who's within?

Enter JESSICA *above, in boy's clothes*

JESSICA Who are you? Tell me for more certainty,
Albeit I'll swear that I do know your tongue.

LORENZO Lorenzo and thy love.

JESSICA Lorenzo certain, and my love indeed,
For who love I so much? And now who knows
But you Lorenzo, whether I am yours?

LORENZO Heaven and thy thoughts are witness that thou art.

JESSICA Here, catch this casket, it is worth the pains.
I am glad 'tis night, you do not look on me,
For I am much ashamed of my exchange.
But love is blind, and lovers cannot see
The pretty follies that themselves commit,
For if they could, Cupid himself would blush
To see me thus transformed to a boy.

LORENZO Descend, for you must be my torch-bearer.

JESSICA What, must I hold a candle to my shames?
They in themselves, good sooth, are too too light.
Why, 'tis an office of discovery, love,
And I should be obscured.

LORENZO So are you, sweet,
Even in the lovely garnish of a boy.
But come at once,
For the close night doth play the runaway,
And we are stayed for at Bassanio's feast.

JESSICA I will make fast the doors, and gild myself

Lorenzo speaks of his love for Jessica. She joins them and they go. Antonio has a message for Gratiano.

50 **moe** more

51 **by my hood** A made-up oath which refers to part of his costume.

gentle A suggestion of the word 'gentile' – she will become one when she converts to Christianity.

52 **Beshrew me** To the devil with me (a mild oath)

62 **Fie, fie** For goodness' sake

63 **stay** are waiting

64 **come about** changed direction

With some moe ducats, and be with you straight.
[*Exit*

GRATIANO Now, by my hood, a gentle and no Jew.

LORENZO Beshrew me but I love her heartily,
For she is wise, if I can judge of her,
And fair she is, if that mine eyes be true,
And true she is, as she hath proved herself;
And therefore like herself, wise, fair, and true,
Shall she be placed in my constant soul.

Enter JESSICA *below*

What, art thou come? On gentlemen, away,
Our masquing mates by this time for us stay.

[*Exit with* JESSICA *and* SALERIO

Enter ANTONIO

ANTONIO Who's there?

GRATIANO Signor Antonio?

ANTONIO Fie, fie Gratiano, where are all the rest?
'Tis nine o'clock, our friends all stay for you.
No masque tonight, the wind is come about;
Bassanio presently will go aboard.
I have sent twenty out to seek for you.

GRATIANO I am glad on't, I desire no more delight
Than to be under sail, and gone tonight.

[*Exeunt*

Act 2 scenes 2 to 6

Playing the fool

The first part of Act 2 scene 2 introduces a character who appears in many of Shakespeare's plays: the Fool. The company of actors Shakespeare wrote for (and with whom he himself acted) always contained one actor who specialised in playing the Fool. The closest thing today is stand-up comic.

The Fool:

- sang songs
- danced
- fooled around
- made things up as he went along
- told rude jokes that weren't in the script.

In this scene we get not just one fool, but two. When the play was first produced, this scene would have been very popular and very funny. The challenge for modern actors and directors is to make it just as funny now. The scene falls into three sections:

	Lines	Characters	What happens
A	1–31	Launcelot	
B	32–109		
C	110–61		

Work on your own

1 Copy out the table and fill in the blanks. In the third column write a short description of what the audience will see: what the speaker does and what the non-speaker does while he is speaking.

Work with a partner

2 Focus on Section A. Launcelot is:

- describing the problem he faces
- acting out a conversation between his conscience and the devil.

3 Take it in turns to act these lines. Try them in different ways. You could for example have Launcelot moving to different positions to speak his conscience's lines and those of the devil.

4 Now discuss how you could act the other sections so as to bring out the humour in them.

Work in a group of four

5 Cast the parts and rehearse lines 1–161.

The elopement

Act 2 scenes 3–6 develop the story of the elopement of Lorenzo and Jessica very quickly. The audience has to concentrate hard to keep up.

Work on your own

1 Read through the scenes again.

2 Sum up what happens in each scene, using a table like this. Only make notes on the lines that tell us about the planned elopement. It has been started for you.

Scene	Characters in scene	Lines	Action
3	Jessica Launcelot	5–9	Jessica hands Launcelot a letter for Lorenzo.
		19–21	
4		10–14	
		19–20	
		29–39	
5		11–16	
		40–3	
6		25–59	

Parents and children

In this section of the play we see two fathers with their children:

- Old Gobbo and Launcelot
- Shylock and Jessica

We can compare how each father treats his child and how the children treat their fathers.

Old Gobbo and Launcelot

Work on your own

1 Look at the list of words and phrases at the bottom of the page. Write down the four that you think best describe the way in which Launcelot treats his father. If you wish, you can use words of your own instead of those in the table.

2 Copy and complete this table:

Chosen **words**	Supporting **evidence** from the text	**Explanation** of why you chose the word

Shylock and Jessica

Work on your own

1 Look at the list of words and phrases at the bottom of the page. Write down the four that you think best describe the way in which Jessica treats Shylock.

2 Use a table like the one above to explain your choices.

3 Now do the same for the way in which Shylock treats Jessica.

Words:

ashamed	bossy	companionable	critical
demanding	disloyal	disobedient	domineering
friendly	hateful	jokey	loving
loyal	mean	obedient	objective
shameful	strict	supportive	teasing
uncaring	unfair	unkind	unloving

Quotation quiz

For each of these quotations, work out:

1 who said it
2 who they were speaking to
3 what it tells us about the speaker and the situation.

The Prince of Morocco comes to choose between the three caskets. He reads the inscriptions and starts to work out their inner meaning. He dismisses straightaway the idea of risking all for lead.

1 **discover** reveal

2 **several** different

8 **all as** just as

9 **hazard** risk

12 **withal** as well

20 **A golden ... dross** A high-minded man is not attracted by what appears worthless

21 **aught** anything

22 **with ... hue** pure white in colour

Scene 7

Belmont

Flourish Cornets. Enter PORTIA *with the* PRINCE OF MOROCCO *and their trains*

PORTIA Go, draw aside the curtains, and discover
The several caskets to this noble prince.
Now make your choice.

MOROCCO This first of gold, who this inscription bears,
'Who chooseth me shall gain what many men desire.'
The second silver, which this promise carries,
'Who chooseth me shall get as much as he deserves.'
This third dull lead, with warning all as blunt,
'Who chooseth me must give and hazard all he hath.'
How shall I know if I do choose the right?

PORTIA The one of them contains my picture Prince:
If you choose that, then I am yours withal.

MOROCCO Some god direct my judgement. Let me see,
I will survey the inscriptions back again.
What says this leaden casket?
'Who chooseth me must give and hazard all he hath.'
Must give – for what? For lead? Hazard for lead?
This casket threatens. Men that hazard all
Do it in hope of fair advantages.
A golden mind stoops not to shows of dross,
I'll then nor give nor hazard aught for lead.
What says the silver with her virgin hue?
'Who chooseth me shall get as much as he deserves.'
As much as he deserves? Pause there Morocco,

He is tempted by the silver inscription because he is sure he deserves Portia, but thinking of her many suitors who desire her, he chooses gold.

25 **with ... hand** fairly, equally

26 **If ... estimation** If you take the value you set on yourself

29–30 **to be ... myself** to underestimate myself would just be a feeble undermining of my own value

32 **in birth** from my social status

33 **In graces** in good looks

36 **graved** engraved

40 **shrine** place of pilgrimage to relics of a saint

41 **Hyrcanian deserts** A region of the ancient Persian Empire next to the Caspian Sea. It had the reputation of being very desolate and full of tigers and snakes.

vasty vast, broad

44 **The watery ... heaven** The sea, whose mountainous waves challenge the sky

47 **As ... brook** as easily as jumping over a stream

50 **base** unworthy (Lead is a base metal, along with copper, zinc, and tin, as opposed to the precious metals, gold, silver, and platinum.)

51 **rib** enclose

cerecloth A wax cloth used to wrap a corpse; a winding-sheet or shroud.

52 **immured** walled up

56 **A coin ... angel** a gold coin showing the archangel Michael piercing the dragon

57 **insculped upon** engraved

60 **thrive ... may** I must be content with my fate whatever it is

And weigh thy value with an even hand.
If thou be'st rated by thy estimation,
Thou dost deserve enough, and yet enough
May not extend so far as to the lady.
And yet to be afeard of my deserving
Were but a weak disabling of myself.
As much as I deserve, why that's the lady.
I do in birth deserve her, and in fortunes,
In graces, and in qualities of breeding;
But more than these, in love I do deserve.
What if I strayed no further, but chose here?
Let's see once more this saying graved in gold:
'Who chooseth me shall gain what many men
desire.'
Why that's the lady, all the world desires her.
From the four corners of the earth they come
To kiss this shrine, this mortal breathing saint.
The Hyrcanian deserts and the vasty wilds
Of wide Arabia are as throughfares now
For princes to come view fair Portia.
The watery kingdom, whose ambitious head
Spits in the face of heaven, is no bar
To stop the foreign spirits, but they come
As o'er a brook to see fair Portia.
One of these three contains her heavenly picture.
Is't like that lead contains her? 'Twere damnation
To think so base a thought; it were too gross
To rib her cerecloth in the obscure grave.
Or shall I think in silver she's immured,
Being ten times undervalued to tried gold?
O sinful thought, never so rich a gem
Was set in worse than gold. They have in England
A coin that bears the figure of an angel
Stamped in gold, but that's insculped upon;
But here an angel in a golden bed
Lies all within. Deliver me the key.
Here do I choose, and thrive I as I may.

Portia's portrait is not in the golden casket. The Prince has failed and leaves.

61 **form** picture

63 **carrion Death** bony skull, death's head

68 **But** just, merely

69 **Gilded ... infold** Tombs and monuments to the dead, which may be covered with gold on the outside will contain the horror of worms

72 **inscrolled** written down in a scroll

73 **suit is cold** courtship is over and done with

77 **tedious** lengthy and formal

part leave, go

78 **A gentle riddance** A gentlemanly parting

79 **complexion** temperament, disposition and colour

In Venice, Salerio and Solanio report Bassanio's departure and Shylock's anger.

PORTIA There, take it Prince, and if my form lie there,
Then I am yours. *[He unlocks the golden casket*

MOROCCO O hell! what have we here?
A carrion Death, within whose empty eye
There is a written scroll. I'll read the writing.

'All that glisters is not gold,
Often have you heard that told.
Many a man his life hath sold
But my outside to behold.
Gilded tombs do worms infold.
Had you been as wise as bold,
Young in limbs, in judgement old,
Your answer had not been inscrolled.
Fare you well, your suit is cold.'

Cold indeed, and labour lost.
Then farewell heat, and welcome frost.

Portia adieu. I have too grieved a heart
To take a tedious leave. Thus losers part.
[Exit with his train

PORTIA A gentle riddance. Draw the curtains, go.
Let all of his complexion choose me so.
[Exeunt

Scene 8

Venice

Enter SALERIO *and* SOLANIO

SALERIO Why man, I saw Bassanio under sail,
With him is Gratiano gone along;
And in their ship I am sure Lorenzo is not.

SOLANIO The villain Jew with outcries raised the duke,
Who went with him to search Bassanio's ship.

SALERIO He came too late, the ship was under sail.
But there the duke was given to understand

Shylock has been seen in the streets lamenting the loss of his daughter and his ducats. There are fears that one of Antonio's ships has been wrecked.

10 **certified** assured

25 **keep his day** repay the loan on time

26 **Marry** Indeed

27 **reasoned** was talking

29 **miscarried** was wrecked

30 **richly fraught** with a valuable cargo

39 **Slubber not** do not hurry over

40 **stay ... time** wait until the right moment

41–2 **And for ... love** as for the question of the bond I pledged to the Jew, do not let it concern you at all in your thoughts of love

That in a gondola were seen together
Lorenzo and his amorous Jessica.
Besides, Antonio certified the duke
They were not with Bassanio in his ship.

SOLANIO I never heard a passion so confused,
So strange, outrageous, and so variable,
As the dog Jew did utter in the streets:
'My daughter! O my ducats! O my daughter!
Fled with a Christian! O my Christian ducats!
Justice! The law! My ducats, and my daughter!
A sealed bag, two sealed bags of ducats,
Of double ducats, stolen from me by my daughter,
And jewels, two stones, two rich and precious
stones,
Stolen by my daughter. Justice! Find the girl!
She hath the stones upon her, and the ducats.'

SALERIO Why, all the boys in Venice follow him,
Crying, his stones, his daughter, and his ducats.

SOLANIO Let good Antonio look he keep his day
Or he shall pay for this.

SALERIO Marry, well remembered.
I reasoned with a Frenchman yesterday
Who told me, in the narrow seas that part
The French and English, there miscarried
A vessel of our country richly fraught.
I thought upon Antonio when he told me,
And wished in silence that it were not his.

SOLANIO You were best to tell Antonio what you hear,
Yet do not suddenly, for it may grieve him.

SALERIO A kinder gentleman treads not the earth.
I saw Bassanio and Antonio part,
Bassanio told him he would make some speed
Of his return. He answered, 'Do not so,
Slubber not business for my sake Bassanio,
But stay the very riping of the time;
And for the Jew's bond which he hath of me,

His friends report the emotional parting of Antonio from Bassanio.

44 **ostents** demonstrations

45 **become you** be fitting for you

46 **even there** at this point

48 **affection wondrous sensible** with such deeply felt emotion

52 **embraced heaviness** this melancholy mood he's taken on

53 **Do we so** Let's do that

At Belmont, the Prince of Arragon is about to make his choice of casket.

1 **straight** straight away

2 **ta'en his oath** taken his oath (at the temple, as we are told in Act 2 scene 1 line 44)

3 **election presently** choice immediately

6 **nuptial rites** wedding ceremony

10 **unfold** disclose

11–12 **fail of** fail to choose

Let it not enter in your mind of love.
Be merry, and employ your chiefest thoughts
To courtship and such fair ostents of love
As shall conveniently become you there.'
And even there, his eye being big with tears,
Turning his face, he put his hand behind him,
And with affection wondrous sensible
He wrung Bassanio's hand; and so they parted.

SOLANIO I think he only loves the world for him.
I pray thee let us go and find him out
And quicken his embraced heaviness
With some delight or other.

SALERIO Do we so.

[*Exeunt*

Scene 9

Belmont

Enter NERISSA *and a Servant*

NERISSA Quick, quick I pray thee, draw the curtain straight.
The Prince of Arragon hath ta'en his oath,
And comes to his election presently.

Flourish Cornets. Enter the PRINCE OF ARRAGON, PORTIA, *and their trains*

PORTIA Behold, there stand the caskets, noble prince.
If you choose that wherein I am contained,
Straight shall our nuptial rites be solemnised;
But if you fail, without more speech my lord,
You must be gone from hence immediately.

ARRAGON I am enjoined by oath to observe three things:
First, never to unfold to any one
Which casket 'twas I chose; next, if I fail
Of the right casket, never in my life
To woo a maid in way of marriage; lastly,

Arragon immediately dismisses the idea of lead. He considers gold and then rejects it. He discusses silver and the concept of 'deserving'.

16 **injunctions** (here) conditions

18 **addressed me** prepared myself

21 **ere** before

26 **fond** foolish

27 **pries not** does not penetrate

martlet house-martin (a bird, similar to a swallow)

29 **in the ... casualty** at risk and in danger of accident

31 **jump** go along with

32 **rank ... multitudes** behave like common people

36 **go about** make an effort

37 **cozen** cheat

38 **stamp** imprint

Without ... merit without really deserving it

40 **estates** status

degrees social rank

offices official positions

41 **derived** acquired, obtained

43 **cover** keep their hats on (as a sign of social status)

45 **gleaned** picked out

45–8 **How ... new-varnished?** Arragon is suggesting here that if people rose only through merit, and not through money or influence, then people pretending to be great would be weeded out and those deserving high office would be rescued from the poor conditions they had been forced into by the way society was organised.

If I do fail in fortune of my choice,
Immediately to leave you and be gone.

PORTIA To these injunctions everyone doth swear
That comes to hazard for my worthless self.

ARRAGON And so have I addressed me – fortune now
To my heart's hope. Gold, silver, and base lead.
'Who chooseth me must give and hazard all he
hath.'
You shall look fairer ere I give or hazard.
What says the golden chest? ha, let me see:
'Who chooseth me shall gain what many men
desire.'
What many men desire – that 'many' may be meant
By the fool multitude that choose by show,
Not learning more than the fond eye doth teach,
Which pries not to the interior, but, like the martlet,
Builds in the weather on the outward wall,
Even in the force and road of casualty.
I will not choose what many men desire,
Because I will not jump with common spirits,
And rank me with the barbarous multitudes.
Why then to thee thou silver treasure-house,
Tell me once more what title thou dost bear:
'Who chooseth me shall get as much as he
deserves'.
And well said too; for who shall go about
To cozen fortune and be honourable
Without the stamp of merit? Let none presume
To wear an undeserved dignity.
O that estates, degrees, and offices,
Were not derived corruptly, and that clear honour
Were purchased by the merit of the wearer.
How many then should cover that stand bare?
How many be commanded that command?
How much low peasantry would then be gleaned
From the true seed of honour, and how much
honour

The Prince of Arragon assumes he deserves the best and chooses silver. He is not successful and leaves.

47 **chaff** the husks left when wheat is threshed

48 **new-varnished** repainted, refurbished

50 **I will ... desert** I will take it for granted that I do deserve Portia

53 **blinking idiot** fool's head (picture of clown or jester)

54 **schedule** statement

60–1 **To ... natures** Portia points out that you can't be judge and defendant at the same time.

62 **tried** refined (as metals are heated to drive off impurities)

64 **amiss** wrongly

65 **that shadows kiss** who kiss shadows (or pictures)

67 **I wis** certainly

68 **Silvered o'er** with white hair (and so supposed to be wise)

69 **Take ... bed** But of course he has promised never to marry if he fails to pick the right casket.

70 **I will ... head** whatever authority you may appear to have, you will always be a fool

71 **sped** finished

76 **adieu** farewell

77 **ruth** sorrow

Picked from the chaff and ruin of the times
To be new-varnished? Well, but to my choice.
'Who chooseth me shall get as much as he
deserves.'
I will assume desert. Give me a key for this,
And instantly unlock my fortunes here.

[*He opens the silver casket*

PORTIA Too long a pause for that which you find there.

ARRAGON What's here? The portrait of a blinking idiot
Presenting me a schedule. I will read it.
How much unlike art thou to Portia.
How much unlike my hopes and my deservings.
'Who chooseth me shall have as much as he
deserves.'
Did I deserve no more than a fool's head?
Is that my prize? Are my deserts no better?

PORTIA To offend and judge are distinct offices
And of opposed natures.

ARRAGON What is here?

'The fire seven times tried this:
Seven times tried that judgement is,
That did never choose amiss.
Some there be that shadows kiss,
Such have but a shadow's bliss.
There be fools alive I wis,
Silvered o'er; and so was this.
Take what wife you will to bed,
I will ever be your head.
So be gone, you are sped.'

Still more fool I shall appear
By the time I linger here.
With one fool's head I came to woo,
But I go away with two.
Sweet adieu. I'll keep my oath,
Patiently to bear my ruth.

[*Exeunt* ARRAGON *and train*

No sooner has Arragon left than the approach of another suitor is announced. Could it be Bassanio?

79 **deliberate fools** fools who spend their time deliberating (that is, considering their choice)

80 **They ... lose** they have just enough sense to get things wrong when they use what sense they have

81 **heresy** false belief

82 **Hanging ... destiny** it's a matter of luck whether you get hanged or married

87 **signify** announce

88 **sensible regreets** substantial greetings (greetings backed up with gifts)

89 **commends** compliments

breath words

93 **costly** lavish, rich

94 **fore-spurrer** horseman who rides ahead of the rest

97 **high-day wit** excited turns of phrase

99 **post** courier, messenger

mannerly courteously

PORTIA Thus hath the candle singed the moth.
O these deliberate fools, when they do choose,
They have the wisdom by their wit to lose.

NERISSA The ancient saying is no heresy,
Hanging and wiving goes by destiny.

PORTIA Come draw the curtain Nerissa.

Enter a SERVANT

SERVANT Where is my lady?

PORTIA Here. What would my lord?

SERVANT Madam, there is alighted at your gate
A young Venetian, one that comes before
To signify th'approaching of his lord;
From whom he bringeth sensible regreets,
To wit, besides commends and courteous breath,
Gifts of rich value. Yet I have not seen
So likely an ambassador of love.
A day in April never came so sweet
To show how costly summer was at hand,
As this fore-spurrer comes before his lord.

PORTIA No more I pray thee, I am half afeard
Thou wilt say anon he is some kin to thee,
Thou spend'st such high-day wit in praising him.
Come, come Nerissa, for I long to see
Quick Cupid's post that comes so mannerly.

NERISSA Bassanio, Lord Love if thy will it be.

[*Exeunt*

Antonio's friends say the rumour is still going around that one of his ships has been wrecked. They hope it is not true. Shylock, meeting them, accuses them of having known about Jessica's elopement.

2 **it ... unchecked** the rumour has not yet been disproved

4 **the Goodwins** The Goodwin Sands, off the Kent coast, were notoriously dangerous to shipping.

5 **carcases** wrecks

6–7 **my gossip Report** my old friend Rumour; an example of **personification** (see Glossary p. 242).

9 **knapped** chewed, munched

11 **without ... prolixity** without slipping into wordiness

11–12 **or crossing ... talk** or abandoning plain speaking

15 **Come, the full stop** Bring it to an end

19 **betimes** quickly

cross prevent from working

Act Three

Scene 1

Venice

Enter SOLANIO *and* SALERIO

SOLANIO Now what news on the Rialto?

SALERIO Why yet it lives there unchecked, that Antonio hath a ship of rich lading wrecked on the narrow seas; the Goodwins I think they call the place, a very dangerous flat, and fatal, where the carcases of many a tall ship lie buried, as they say, if my gossip Report be an honest woman of her word.

SOLANIO I would she were as lying a gossip in that as ever knapped ginger, or made her neighbours believe she wept for the death of a third husband. But it is true, without any slips of prolixity, or crossing the plain highway of talk, that the good Antonio, the honest Antonio – O that I had a title good enough to keep his name company –

SALERIO Come, the full stop.

SOLANIO Ha, what sayest thou? Why, the end is, he hath lost a ship.

SALERIO I would it might prove the end of his losses.

SOLANIO Let me say 'amen' betimes, lest the devil cross my prayer, for here he comes in the likeness of a Jew.

Enter SHYLOCK

How now Shylock, what news among the merchants?

SHYLOCK You knew, none so well, none so well as you, of my daughter's flight.

Shylock, while angry and hurt at Jessica's departure, makes it clear he will take revenge on Antonio if he defaults. He speaks passionately of Jews' and Christians' common humanity.

26 **wings ... withal** the page's costume she escaped in

28 **fledged** ready to fly the nest

complexion nature, temperament

29 **dam** mother (bird); Shylock makes a **play on words** when he uses 'damned' in line 30 (see Glossary p. 242).

32 **My ... blood** My child

33 **Out upon it** (expression of disgust)

carrion rotting flesh, carcass

rebels ... years Solanio and Salerio are being deliberately unpleasant. They take Shylock's words to mean that 'even at his age' he has uncontrollable sexual urges.

36 **jet** A black mineral.

37 **rhenish** Rhine wine, a fine white wine

40 **match** deal

42 **smug** Originally meant 'smart', 'neatly dressed'. At about the time Shakespeare was writing this play, the meaning was changing to include 'complacent'. Either or both meanings would fit well here.

43 **mart** market, the exchange

45–6 **for ... courtesy** at no charge because he was a Christian

51 **hindered me** prevented my making

52 **my nation** i.e. the Jews

52–3 **thwarted my bargains** spoiled my deals

56 **dimensions** (human) proportions

SALERIO That's certain. I for my part knew the tailor that made the wings she flew withal.

SOLANIO And Shylock for his own part knew the bird was fledged, and then it is the complexion of them all to leave the dam.

SHYLOCK She is damned for it.

SALERIO That's certain, if the devil may be her judge.

SHYLOCK My own flesh and blood to rebel.

SOLANIO Out upon it old carrion, rebels it at these years?

SHYLOCK I say my daughter is my flesh and my blood.

SALERIO There is more difference between thy flesh and hers, than between jet and ivory; more between your bloods, than there is between red wine and rhenish. But tell us, do you hear whether Antonio have had any loss at sea or no?

SHYLOCK There I have another bad match, a bankrupt, a prodigal, who dare scarce show his head on the Rialto, a beggar, that was used to come so smug upon the mart. Let him look to his bond. He was wont to call me usurer, let him look to his bond. He was wont to lend money for a Christian courtesy, let him look to his bond.

SALERIO Why I am sure, if he forfeit, thou wilt not take his flesh, what's that good for?

SHYLOCK To bait fish withal. If it will feed nothing else, it will feed my revenge. He hath disgraced me, and hindered me half a million, laughed at my losses, mocked at my gains, scorned my nation, thwarted my bargains, cooled my friends, heated mine enemies, and what's his reason? I am a Jew. Hath not a Jew eyes? Hath not a Jew hands, organs, dimensions, senses, affections, passions? Fed with the same food, hurt with the same weapons, subject to the same diseases, healed by the same means, warmed and cooled by the same winter and

Shylock continues to insist on revenge. When Solanio and Salerio leave, Tubal reports to Shylock on his search for Jessica.

65 **what is his humility?** The Christian teaching is to accept wrongs with humility. Shylock suggests that Christians do not practise what they preach, but want revenge.

66 **sufferance** toleration, endurance

68 **execute** carry out

68–9 **it shall ... I will** I will most certainly

69 **better the instruction** improve on what I have been taught (by Christians)

73–4 **cannot be matched** cannot be found to compare with them

80 **curse** See Deuteronomy 28, verses 15 onwards. This is a long list of curses afflicting every imaginable aspect of life, which God threatens will fall upon the Jews if they do not follow all his commandments.

85 **hearsed** in her coffin

90 **lights** settles

summer, as a Christian is? If you prick us do we not bleed? If you tickle us do we not laugh? If you poison us do we not die? And if you wrong us shall we not revenge? If we are like you in the rest, we will resemble you in that. If a Jew wrong a Christian, what is his humility? Revenge. If a Christian wrong a Jew, what should his sufferance be by Christian example? Why revenge. The villainy you teach me I will execute, and it shall go hard but I will better the instruction.

Enter a SERVANT

SERVANT Gentlemen, my master Antonio is at his house, and desires to speak with you both.

SALERIO We have been up and down to seek him.

Enter TUBAL

SOLANIO Here comes another of the tribe; a third cannot be matched, unless the devil himself turn Jew.

[*Exeunt* SOLANIO, SALERIO, *and* SERVANT

SHYLOCK How now Tubal, what news from Genoa? Hast thou found my daughter?

TUBAL I often came where I did hear of her, but cannot find her.

SHYLOCK Why there, there, there, there, a diamond gone cost me two thousand ducats in Frankfort. The curse never fell upon our nation till now, I never felt it till now. Two thousand ducats in that, and other precious, precious jewels. I would my daughter were dead at my foot, and the jewels in her ear. Would she were hearsed at my foot, and the ducats in her coffin. No news of them? Why so – and I know not what's spent in the search. Why, thou – loss upon loss. The thief gone with so much, and so much to find the thief, and no satisfaction, no revenge, nor no ill luck stirring but what lights

Tubal has heard of the loss of a second ship of Antonio's. He also tells of Jessica's spending spree. Shylock starts to make arrangements for the forfeit of Antonio's bond.

96 **cast away** wrecked

103 **fourscore** eighty

107 **divers … creditors** several men to whom Antonio owes money

109 **break** fail, go bankrupt

115 **Leah** presumably Shylock's wife, now dead

119–20 **fee … officer** pay for an arresting officer for me

120 **bespeak him** book him, engage him

before before the date when the loan is due to be repaid

121–2 **were … I will** if he were removed from Venice I could make whatever deals I chose on my shoulders, no sighs but of my breathing, no tears but of my shedding.

TUBAL Yes, other men have ill luck too. Antonio, as I heard in Genoa –

SHYLOCK What, what, what? Ill luck, ill luck?

TUBAL Hath an argosy cast away coming from Tripolis.

SHYLOCK I thank God, I thank God. Is it true, is it true?

TUBAL I spoke with some of the sailors that escaped the wreck.

SHYLOCK I thank thee good Tubal, good news, good news! Ha, ha! Heard in Genoa?

TUBAL Your daughter spent in Genoa, as I heard, one night fourscore ducats.

SHYLOCK Thou stick'st a dagger in me. I shall never see my gold again. Fourscore ducats at a sitting, fourscore ducats.

TUBAL There came divers of Antonio's creditors in my company to Venice, that swear he cannot choose but break.

SHYLOCK I am very glad of it, I'll plague him, I'll torture him. I am glad of it.

TUBAL One of them showed me a ring that he had of your daughter for a monkey.

SHYLOCK Out upon her, thou torturest me Tubal. It was my turquoise, I had it of Leah when I was a bachelor. I would not have given it for a wilderness of monkeys.

TUBAL But Antonio is certainly undone.

SHYLOCK Nay, that's true, that's very true. Go Tubal, fee me an officer; bespeak him a fortnight before. I will have the heart of him if he forfeit, for were he out of Venice, I can make what merchandise I will. Go Tubal, and meet me at our synagogue. Go good Tubal, at our synagogue Tubal.

[*Exeunt*

Act 2 scenes 7 to 9; Act 3 scene 1

The casket challenge

In Act 2 scenes 7 and 9 we see how the Prince of Morocco and the Prince of Arragon face the challenge of choosing the right casket to win Portia's hand in marriage. Each tackles the challenge differently – and both lose.

Work on your own

1 Copy out the chart below.

2 Read the two scenes again and fill in the spaces in the chart. It has been started for you.

The casket	Morocco's thoughts	Arragon's thoughts	The contents
Material: *Gold* Inscription:	For: Against:	For: Against:	*Skull and scroll*
Material: Inscription: *'Who chooseth me shall get as much as he deserves'*	For: Against:	For: Against:	
Material: Inscription:	For: Against: *Why risk everything for lead? The lady deserves more.*	For: Against:	

3 When you have finished, share your answers with a partner.

Scene 8: action off-stage

This scene adds several episodes to the story, but none of them is shown on stage. Instead they are described in a conversation between Salerio and Solanio. In a modern film or TV version of the play, these parts of the story could be handled in different ways. For example, instead of describing the shipwreck (lines 27–30), it could be shown on screen, with Salerio's voice speaking the lines.

Work with a partner

1 Read again lines 1–24.

2 Discuss how you might film these lines, using Shakespeare's words, but showing some or all of the events described as they happen.

3 Divide these lines into shorter sections and work out what you would show in each section, as Salerio and Solanio say their lines.

4 Make a storyboard setting out your ideas. This one has been started for you:

Lines	Location	Visual	Action
1–3	The harbour		Bassanio and Gratiano stand on the side of a ship, waving goodbye, as it sets sail and begins to move away from the jetty.
4	The Duke's palace		Shylock pleads with the Duke for justice. The Duke finally agrees.
5			

Shylock's mood

Shylock begins Act 3 scene 1 grieving and angry at the behaviour of his daughter Jessica. 'She is damned for it', he says (line 30). By the end of the scene he is exulting at the downfall of Antonio:

I will have the heart of him if he forfeit, for were he out of Venice, I can make what merchandise I will. (lines 120–2)

In between these two points, Shylock's mood shifts to and fro. You can plot this on a mood temperature chart. It might start like this:

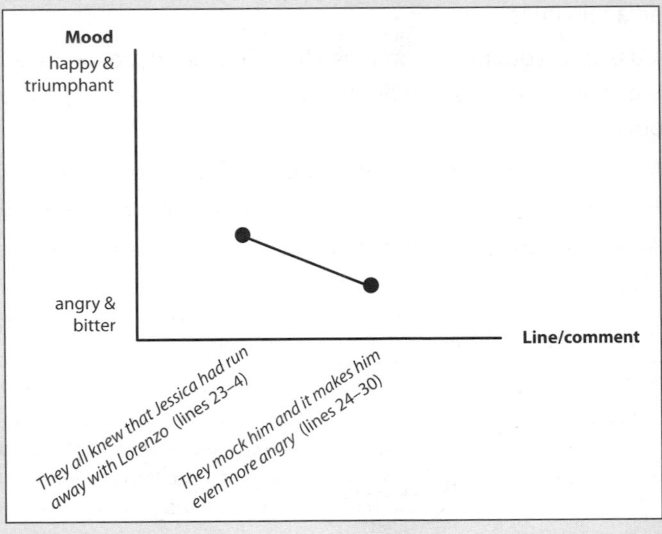

Work on your own

1. Copy out the chart onto a large sheet of paper. Make sure that you have plenty of space from left to right: Shylock's mood changes a lot!
2. Along the lower axis mark the points at which his mood changes. Write down:
   - a short description of how and why his mood changes
   - the line numbers where this happens.
3. Mark on the graph where his mood is on the scale from 'angry & bitter' to 'happy & triumphant', and join up the points you have marked.

Quotation quiz

For each of these quotations, work out:

1 who said it

2 who they were speaking to

3 what it tells us about:

  a the speaker

  b the situation

  c any other characters.

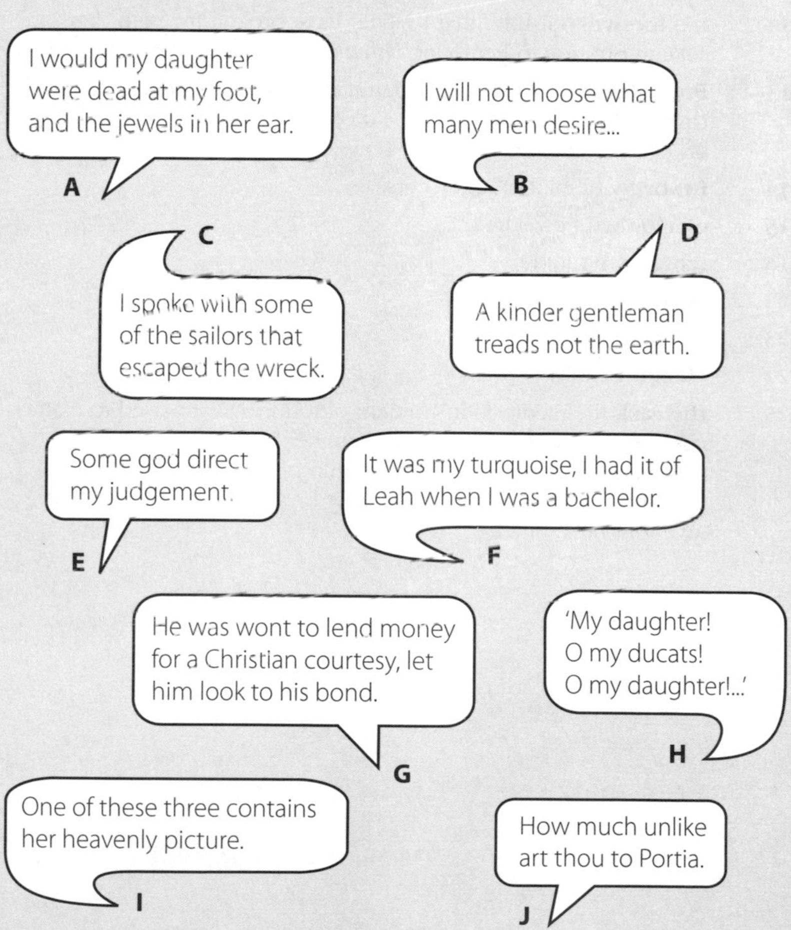

Portia, in danger of giving away her feelings for Bassanio, asks him to delay choosing. He cannot bear to wait.

1 **tarry** delay

3 **forbear** hold off, wait

6 **Hate ... quality** if I hated you I wouldn't speak to you like this

7 **lest** in case

8 **And ... thought** a girl is not supposed to speak her thoughts on the subject of love

10 **venture** take your chance

11 **I ... forsworn** if I did that I would have broken my oath (her solemn promise to her dying father)

13–14 **But ... forsworn** Portia says that if Bassanio fails to make the right choice, he'll make her wish she'd committed a sin – that she had broken her oath and told him how to choose.

14 **Beshrew** (a mild or jokey curse)

15 **o'erlooked** bewitched

18 **naughty** wicked

22 **peize** weigh down

23 **eke** make it last

24 **election** choice

25 **the rack** the medieval instrument of torture; it was used to extract confessions particularly from people held for treason. In the following 14 lines Portia and Bassanio play with the ideas of forced confession, of mistrust and of loyalty. They confess their love for one another.

Scene 2

Belmont

Enter BASSANIO, PORTIA, GRATIANO, NERISSA, *and Attendants*

PORTIA
I pray you tarry, pause a day or two
Before you hazard, for in choosing wrong
I lose your company; therefore forbear awhile.
There's something tells me – but it is not love –
I would not lose you, and you know yourself
Hate counsels not in such a quality.
But lest you should not understand me well –
And yet a maiden hath no tongue but thought –
I would detain you here some month or two
Before you venture for me. I could teach you
How to choose right, but I am then forsworn;
So will I never be, so may you miss me;
But if you do, you'll make me wish a sin,
That I had been forsworn. Beshrew your eyes,
They have o'erlooked me, and divided me;
One half of me is yours, the other half yours –
Mine own I would say, but if mine then yours,
And so all yours. O these naughty times
Puts bars between the owners and their rights.
And so though yours, not yours. Prove it so.
Let fortune go to hell for it, not I.
I speak too long, but 'tis to peize the time,
To eke it, and to draw it out in length,
To stay you from election.

BASSANIO
Let me choose,
For as I am, I live upon the rack.

PORTIA
Upon the rack Bassanio then confess
What treason there is mingled with your love.

BASSANIO
None but that ugly treason of mistrust,

Portia orders music while Bassanio makes his choice: it will be a swan-song if he fails, a fanfare if he wins her.

30 **amity** friendship

36 **Had ... sum** would have been the total amount

38 **Doth ... deliverance** teaches me the answers I should give to make the torture stop

42 **all aloof** some distance away

44 **a swan-like end** The ancient belief was that a swan would sing just before its death.

49 **flourish** fanfare

51 **dulcet** sweet

55 **Alcides** one of the names for Hercules or Herakles (he was the grandson of Alcaeus). Lines 53–61 refer to a story about him: the King of Troy, Laomedon, had his daughter Hesione chained to a rock. She was to be torn apart and devoured by a sea monster as an offering to the gods he had offended. Hercules rescued her, and killed the monster, not for love, but for the promised reward of six fine horses, which he did not receive.

56 **virgin tribute** sacrifice of Hesione, daughter of the King of Troy

58 **Dardanian wives** Trojan women

59 **bleared** tear-stained

60 **issue** result

62 **fray** fight

Which makes me fear the enjoying of my love.
There may as well be amity and life
'Tween snow and fire, as treason and my love.

PORTIA Ay but I fear you speak upon the rack
Where men enforced do speak anything.

BASSANIO Promise me life, and I'll confess the truth.

PORTIA Well then, confess and live.

BASSANIO 'Confess' and 'love'
Had been the very sum of my confession.
O happy torment, when my torturer
Doth teach me answers for deliverance.
But let me to my fortune and the caskets.

PORTIA Away then, I am locked in one of them,
If you do love me, you will find me out.
Nerissa and the rest, stand all aloof,
Let music sound while he doth make his choice;
Then if he lose he makes a swan-like end,
Fading in music. That the comparison
May stand more proper, my eye shall be the stream
And watery death-bed for him. He may win,
And what is music then? Then music is
Even as the flourish, when true subjects bow
To a new-crowned monarch. Such it is
As are those dulcet sounds in break of day
That creep into the dreaming bridegroom's ear
And summon him to marriage. Now he goes
With no less presence, but with much more love,
Than young Alcides, when he did redeem
The virgin tribute paid by howling Troy
To the sea-monster. I stand for sacrifice;
The rest aloof are the Dardanian wives,
With bleared visages come forth to view
The issue of th' exploit. Go Hercules.
Live thou, I live. With much much more dismay
I view the fight than thou that mak'st the fray.

While the song is being sung, Bassanio expresses his thoughts on areas of life where the external appearance can hide something much less attractive: the law, religion, bravery, beauty.

SD ***comments ... himself*** considers the inscriptions silently

63 **fancy** love, attraction

65 **begot** created

67 **It is engendered** It comes into being (The song suggests that if love is only based on sight, on the outward show, it will not last very long.)

70 **knell** tolling bell that is rung when someone dies

74 **still** continually

75 **tainted** contaminated (The metaphor is of tainted food, particularly meat which, when it was going off, needed seasoning or spices to mask the bad flavour.)

78 **sober brow** serious person

79 **approve it** demonstrate it to be true

86 **livers ... milk** without red blood and so white, cowardly

87 **these** these men

valour's excrement beards, an outward show of bravery

88 **redoubted** feared

89 **purchased ... weight** cosmetics were bought by weight; the 'miracle' which Bassanio speaks of, is that those women who wear most (weight of) make-up are also the 'lightest'. The **play on words** here (see Glossary p. 242) is that 'light' also means 'frivolous' or 'immoral'.

92 **crisped** curled

93 **Which ... wind** which play so lovingly with the wind

94 **Upon supposed fairness** pretending beauty

95 **dowry** money and goods which a bride brought to her husband (here used in the sense of 'legacy')

96 **The skull ... sepulchre** the head on which the hair had grown, now a skull in the tomb (Hair was sold to be made into wigs.)

A song to music whilst BASSANIO *comments on the caskets to himself*

Tell me where is fancy bred,
Or in the heart or in the head?
How begot, how nourished?

ALL Reply, reply.

It is engendered in the eyes,
With gazing fed; and fancy dies
In the cradle where it lies.
Let us all ring fancy's knell;
I'll begin it, ding, dong, bell.

ALL Ding, dong, bell.

BASSANIO So may the outward shows be least themselves.
The world is still deceived with ornament.
In law, what plea so tainted and corrupt
But being seasoned with a gracious voice,
Obscures the show of evil? In religion,
What damned error but some sober brow
Will bless it, and approve it with a text,
Hiding the grossness with fair ornament?
There is no vice so simple, but assumes
Some mark of virtue on his outward parts.
How many cowards whose hearts are all as false
As stairs of sand, wear yet upon their chins
The beards of Hercules and frowning Mars,
Who inward searched, have livers white as milk?
And these assume but valour's excrement
To render them redoubted. Look on beauty,
And you shall see 'tis purchased by the weight,
Which therein works a miracle in nature,
Making them lightest that wear most of it.
So are those crisped snaky golden locks
Which make such wanton gambols with the wind
Upon supposed fairness, often known
To be the dowry of a second head,
The skull that bred them in the sepulchre.

As a result of his deliberations Bassanio chooses the least showy casket – lead. Portia and Bassanio are delighted that he has chosen the correct casket.

97 **guiled** treacherous

100 **seeming** apparent

102 **Hard ... Midas** King Midas, given one wish as a reward by Dionysus, asked that everything he touched be turned to gold. He soon found he couldn't eat gold.

103 **palled** over-used, boring

common drudge everyone's servant (Silver was used for coins, and so served everyone.)

108 **fleet to air** evaporate

109 **As** such as

rash-embraced too quickly adopted

110 **jealousy** mistrust

111 **allay** reduce

112 **measure** moderation

rain pour

scant tone down

115 **counterfeit** portrait

117–18 **Or ... motion?** Or is it because my eyes are looking at them, they seem to move?

118 **severed** parted

120 **sunder** part

123 **Faster** more securely

124–6 **Having ... unfurnished** Once he had painted one of her eyes so beautifully the painter would only be able to gaze at it and so be unable to paint the other one

126–9 **Yet ... substance** See to what extent the wealth of my praise does not do justice to the picture because it undervalues it; to the same extent the picture is nowhere near the original (Portia herself)

127 **substance** wealth

130 **continent** store

Thus ornament is but the guiled shore
To a most dangerous sea, the beauteous scarf
Veiling an Indian beauty; in a word,
The seeming truth which cunning times put on
To entrap the wisest. Therefore thou gaudy gold,
Hard food for Midas, I will none of thee.
Nor none of thee, thou palled and common drudge
'Tween man and man. But thou, thou meagre lead
Which rather threatenest than dost promise aught,
Thy paleness moves me more than eloquence,
And here choose I, joy be the consequence.

PORTIA [*Aside*] How all the other passions fleet to air,
As doubtful thoughts, and rash-embraced despair,
And shuddering fear, and green-eyed jealousy.
O love be moderate, allay thy ecstasy,
In measure rain thy joy, scant this excess.
I feel too much thy blessing, make it less
For fear I surfeit.

BASSANIO What find I here?

[*He opens the leaden casket*

Fair Portia's counterfeit. What demi-god
Hath come so near creation? Move these eyes?
Or whether riding on the balls of mine
Seem they in motion? Here are severed lips
Parted with sugar breath, so sweet a bar
Should sunder such sweet friends. Here in her hairs
The painter plays the spider, and hath woven
A golden mesh t'entrap the hearts of men
Faster than gnats in cobwebs: but her eyes –
How could he see to do them? Having made one,
Methinks it should have power to steal both his
And leave itself unfurnished. Yet look how far
The substance of my praise doth wrong this shadow
In underprizing it, so far this shadow
Doth limp behind the substance. Here's the scroll,
The continent and summary of my fortune.

Bassanio reads his scroll and turns to Portia to claim his kiss. She happily offers all she is, and has, to him.

140 **by note** by this account ('Note' is both a bill, and a reference to the scroll.)

141–8 **Like ... by you** Bassanio compares himself to someone competing with one other in a sport. He hears the applause and thinks he has won, but he can't be sure until he is told it is so.

148 **ratified** confirmed

155 **account** opinion

156 **livings** possessions

157 **account** reckoning, counting up

158 **term in gross** describe in full

167 **But now** A moment ago

'You that choose not by the view,
Chance as fair and choose as true.
Since this fortune falls to you,
Be content and seek no new.
If you be well pleased with this
And hold your fortune for your bliss,
Turn you where your lady is,
And claim her with a loving kiss.'

A gentle scroll. Fair lady, by your leave.
I come by note to give, and to receive.
Like one of two contending in a prize
That thinks he hath done well in people's eyes,
Hearing applause and universal shout,
Giddy in spirit, still gazing in a doubt
Whether those peals of praise be his or no,
So thrice-fair lady stand I even so,
As doubtful whether what I see be true,
Until confirmed, signed, ratified by you.

PORTIA You see me Lord Bassanio where I stand,
Such as I am. Though for myself alone
I would not be ambitious in my wish,
To wish myself much better, yet for you,
I would be trebled twenty times myself,
A thousand times more fair, ten thousand times
More rich, that only to stand high in your account,
I might in virtues, beauties, livings, friends,
Exceed account. But the full sum of me
Is sum of nothing; which to term in gross,
Is an unlessoned girl, unschooled, unpractised,
Happy in this, she is not yet so old
But she may learn; happier than this,
She is not bred so dull but she can learn;
Happiest of all, is that her gentle spirit
Commits itself to yours to be directed,
As from her lord, her governor, her king.
Myself, and what is mine, to you and yours
Is now converted. But now I was the lord
Of this fair mansion, master of my servants,

Portia gives Bassanio a ring to confirm that they will marry. He is never to part with it. Nerissa and Gratiano congratulate them. They have also fallen in love and wish to marry.

169 **even now, but now** from this very moment

173 **presage** foretell

174 **vantage** opportunity

exclaim on protest to, reproach

175 **bereft me** robbed me

178 **oration** formal speech

181 **blent** blended

182 **wild of nothing** a confused din

192–3 **solemnise ... faith** marry to confirm your loving agreement

194 **Even ... time** at that very time

195 **so** assuming that

199 **intermission** delay

200 **No ... me** is no more part of my nature

203 **sweat** (past tense) sweated

204 **roof** (of his mouth, dry because his future happiness depended on his master's making the right choice)

Queen o'er myself. And even now, but now,
This house, these servants and this same myself
Are yours – my lord's – I give them with this ring,
Which when you part from, lose, or give away,
Let it presage the ruin of your love,
And be my vantage to exclaim on you.

BASSANIO Madam, you have bereft me of all words,
Only my blood speaks to you in my veins,
And there is such confusion in my powers,
As after some oration fairly spoke
By a beloved prince, there doth appear
Among the buzzing pleased multitude,
Where every something, being blent together,
Turns to a wild of nothing, save of joy
Expressed, and not expressed. But when this ring
Parts from this finger, then parts life from hence:
O then be bold to say Bassanio's dead.

NERISSA My lord and lady, it is now our time
That have stood by and seen our wishes prosper,
To cry 'good joy', Good joy my lord and lady.

GRATIANO My lord Bassanio and my gentle lady,
I wish you all the joy that you can wish,
For I am sure you can wish none from me.
And when your honours mean to solemnise
The bargain of your faith, I do beseech you
Even at that time I may be married too.

BASSANIO With all my heart, so thou canst get a wife.

GRATIANO I thank your lordship, you have got me one.
My eyes my lord can look as swift as yours:
You saw the mistress, I beheld the maid.
You loved, I loved, for intermission
No more pertains to me my lord than you.
Your fortune stood upon the caskets there,
And so did mine too as the matter falls.
For wooing here until I sweat again,
And swearing till my very roof was dry

The double wedding is promised. Visitors arrive from Venice.

205 **oaths** solemn promises

209 **so ... withal** if this is acceptable to you

213–14 **We'll ... ducats** Gratiano wants to bet on which couple will be the first to produce a son.

215–17 **stake down a play on words** (see Glossary p. 242): 1) with your money on the table 2) without an erection.

218 **infidel** unbeliever (Jessica has presumably not had time to convert to Christianity.)

221 **the youth ... here** Bassanio is aware that he has only just won the right to marry Portia.

229 **past ... nay** and it was impossible to refuse him

With oaths of love, at last, if promise last,
I got a promise of this fair one here
To have her love, provided that your fortune
Achieved her mistress.

PORTIA Is this true Nerissa?

NERISSA Madam it is, so you stand pleased withal.

BASSANIO And do you Gratiano mean good faith?

GRATIANO Yes faith, my lord.

BASSANIO Our feast shall be much honoured in your marriage.

GRATIANO We'll play with them the first boy for a thousand ducats.

NERISSA What, and stake down?

GRATIANO No, we shall ne'er win at that sport, and stake down.

BASSANIO But who comes here? Lorenzo and his infidel?
What, and my old Venetian friend Salerio?

Enter LORENZO, JESSICA, *and* SALERIO, *a messenger from Venice*

BASSANIO Lorenzo and Salerio, welcome hither,
If that the youth of my new interest here
Have power to bid you welcome. By your leave,
I bid my very friends and countrymen,
Sweet Portia, welcome.

PORTIA So do I my lord,
They are entirely welcome.

LORENZO I thank your honour. For my part my lord,
My purpose was not to have seen you here,
But meeting with Salerio by the way
He did entreat me past all saying nay
To come with him along.

SALERIO I did my lord,
And I have reason for it. Signor Antonio
Commends him to you. [*Gives* BASSANIO *a letter*

Gratiano's mood does not fit with the news of Antonio. As Bassanio starts to read the letter Portia perceives that it contains really bad news. Bassanio admits the sad state of his affairs and his debt to Antonio.

232 **Ere I ope** Before I open

236 **his estate** his condition, the state of affairs with him

237 **cheer** greet

yond stranger that visitor (Jessica)

241 **We ... fleece** Gratiano, with his usual lack of sensitivity, boasts of their success. For the reference to the Jason story, see note on Act 1 scene 1 lines 170–2 (p. 12).

242 **I would ... lost** With a punning reference (for **pun** see Glossary p. 242) to 'fleece'/'fleets', Salerio points up Antonio's disastrous situation.

243 **shrewd contents** bad news ('Shrewd' meant 'evil'.)

245 **else** otherwise

246–7 **turn ... man** so affect the mood of a balanced man

252 **blotted** stained

253 **impart ... you** tell you I loved you

258 **How ... braggart** how boastful I was being

259 **state** estate, property

261 **engaged** bound, pledged

262 **mere** absolute

263 **feed my means** supply me with money

BASSANIO Ere I ope his letter
I pray you tell me how my good friend doth.

SALERIO Not sick my lord, unless it be in mind,
Nor well, unless in mind. His letter there
Will show you his estate. [BASSANIO *opens the letter*

GRATIANO Nerissa, cheer yond stranger, bid her welcome.
Your hand Salerio, what's the news from Venice?
How doth that royal merchant, good Antonio?
I know he will be glad of our success.
We are the Jasons, we have won the fleece.

SALERIO I would you had won the fleece that he hath lost.

PORTIA There are some shrewd contents in yond same paper
That steals the colour from Bassanio's cheek.
Some dear friend dead, else nothing in the world
Could turn so much the constitution
Of any constant man. What, worse and worse?
With leave Bassanio, I am half yourself,
And I must freely have the half of anything
That this same paper brings you.

BASSANIO O sweet Portia,
Here are a few of the unpleasant'st words
That ever blotted paper. Gentle lady,
When I did first impart my love to you,
I freely told you all the wealth I had
Ran in my veins – I was a gentleman,
And then I told you true. And yet dear lady,
Rating myself at nothing, you shall see
How much I was a braggart. When I told you
My state was nothing, I should then have told you
That I was worse than nothing; for indeed
I have engaged myself to a dear friend,
Engaged my friend to his mere enemy,
To feed my means. Here is a letter lady;
The paper as the body of my friend,
And every word in it a gaping wound

The letter tells that all Antonio's ships are wrecked. Shylock is demanding his bond and would not accept money even if it were available. Bassanio praises Antonio.

266 **Issuing life-blood** with his life bleeding away

267 **hit** succeeded

269 **Barbary** the North African coast

271 **merchant-marring** ship-breaking

273 **present money** ready money

discharge pay off

276 **keen** sharp

confound destroy

277 **plies** appeals to, petitions

278–9 **doth ... justice** accuses the state of not holding to its own laws if he is denied justice

280 **magnificoes** chief citizens of Venice

281 **port** status

persuaded pleaded

282 **envious** malicious

293 **The best-conditioned** with the best qualities

293–4 **unwearied ... courtesies** never tired of doing kindnesses

Issuing life-blood. But is it true Salerio?
Have all his ventures failed? What not one hit?
From Tripolis, from Mexico and England,
From Lisbon, Barbary and India?
And not one vessel 'scape the dreadful touch
Of merchant-marring rocks?

SALERIO Not one, my lord.
Besides, it should appear, that if he had
The present money to discharge the Jew,
He would not take it. Never did I know
A creature that did bear the shape of man
So keen and greedy to confound a man.
He plies the duke at morning and at night,
And doth impeach the freedom of the state
If they deny him justice. Twenty merchants,
The duke himself, and the magnificoes
Of greatest port have all persuaded with him,
But none can drive him from the envious plea
Of forfeiture, of justice, and his bond.

JESSICA When I was with him, I have heard him swear
To Tubal and to Chus, his countrymen,
That he would rather have Antonio's flesh
Than twenty times the value of the sum
That he did owe him. And I know my lord,
If law, authority, and power deny not,
It will go hard with poor Antonio.

PORTIA Is it your dear friend that is thus in trouble?

BASSANIO The dearest friend to me, the kindest man,
The best-conditioned and unwearied spirit
In doing courtesies; and one in whom
The ancient Roman honour more appears
Than any that draws breath in Italy.

PORTIA What sum owes he the Jew?

Portia offers any amount of money to save Bassanio's friend. They shall marry straight away but then Bassanio must go directly to Venice.

299 **deface** cancel

306 **unquiet** anxious

312 **a merry cheer** a cheerful face

313 **Since ... bought** just as your friend (Antonio) has risked everything for you

316 **miscarried** come to harm

323 **dispatch** settle

326–7 **No ... twain** Bassanio will not let either sleep or rest come between him and Portia till his return.

BASSANIO For me three thousand ducats.

PORTIA What, no more?
Pay him six thousand, and deface the bond;
Double six thousand, and then treble that,
Before a friend of this description
Shall lose a hair through Bassanio's fault.
First go with me to church, and call me wife,
And then away to Venice to your friend.
For never shall you lie by Portia's side
With an unquiet soul. You shall have gold
To pay the petty debt twenty times over.
When it is paid, bring your true friend along.
My maid Nerissa and myself meantime
Will live as maids and widows. Come away
For you shall hence upon your wedding day.
Bid your friends welcome, show a merry cheer,
Since you are dear bought, I will love you dear.
But let me hear the letter of your friend.

BASSANIO [*Reads*] 'Sweet Bassanio, my ships have all miscarried, my creditors grow cruel, my estate is very low, my bond to the Jew is forfeit, and since in paying it, it is impossible I should live, all debts are cleared between you and I if I might but see you at my death. Notwithstanding, use your pleasure; if your love do not persuade you to come, let not my letter.'

PORTIA O love, dispatch all business and be gone.

BASSANIO Since I have your good leave to go away,
I will make haste; but till I come again,
No bed shall e'er be guilty of my stay,
Nor rest be interposer 'twixt us twain.

[*Exeunt*

Act 3 scene 2

Staging the casket scene

This is a long and detailed scene. As we read it, it is important to get a clear picture of:

- what is going on
- how it would have been staged in Shakespeare's theatre.

Work on your own

1 Copy and complete this table. It has been started for you:

Lines	Characters who speak	Other characters on stage	The main things that happen
1–42	Portia, Bassanio		
43–62			
63–72			While Bassanio looks at the caskets, the others sing the song.
73–148			
149–185			

Work with a partner

2 Discuss your answers in the table.

3 Now look at the pictures of Shakespeare's theatre on pages xiii–xvi and think about how Act 3 scene 2 could have been staged. For example, where are the caskets placed and how do they get there? Who is on stage and how do they get there?

4 Copy the stage diagram at the top of the next page. Choose the first of the five sections in your table. Mark on the diagram where everyone is standing.

5 Now do the same for the other sections.

6 Present your ideas to the rest of the class.

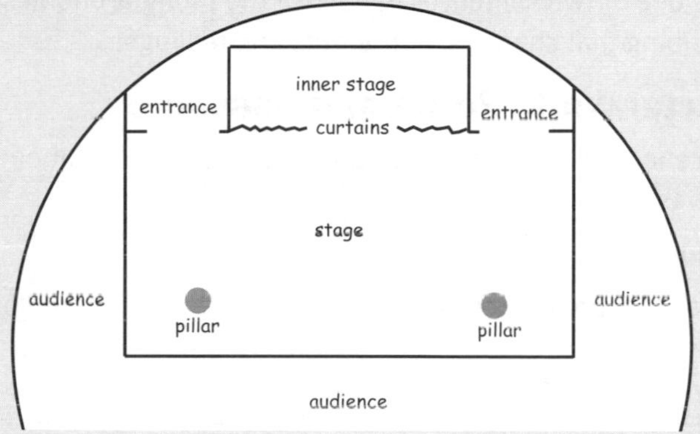

Thought-plotting

There is a dramatic moment in this same scene, when Salerio brings news that all Antonio's ships have been wrecked. Bassanio asks him if not even one of them has survived. Salerio replies, 'Not one, my lord'. At this point different characters will react in different ways according to:

- how much they know about Antonio
- how they are affected personally by this news.

Work on your own

1 Copy out this diagram onto a large sheet of paper.

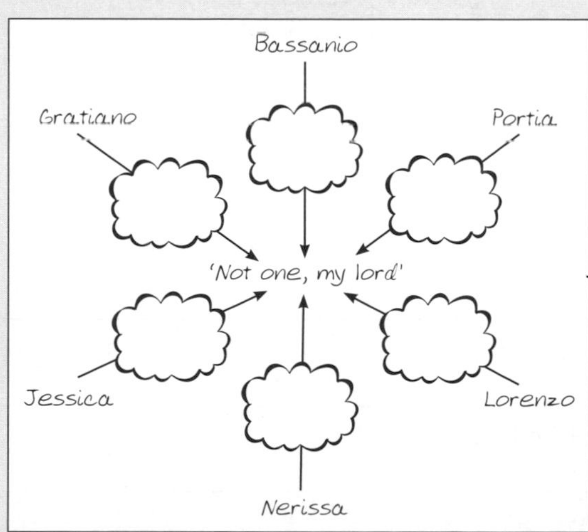

2 Think about what each of the characters in the scene would have thought and felt when they heard these words.

3 Write one or two sentences in each of the thought bubbles describing that character's thoughts and feelings.

Character work: Portia and Bassanio

In this scene both Portia and Bassanio reveal quite a lot about themselves.

Work with a partner

1 In the table below, key sections of text have been picked out. Each illustrates features of Portia's character. Copy and complete the table.

Lines	What they mean	What they tell us about her
1–5	She wants him to wait a day or two before making his decision. She doesn't want to lose him, but not because she loves him.	She doesn't want to face up to how she would feel if he made the wrong choice, or admit even to herself that she loves him.
10–14	She could tell him the right answer but that would mean breaking her solemn promise. So he may choose wrongly, which would make her wish she had told him – and that would have been a sin.	
60–2		
111–14		
157–65		
170–1		

2 Now do the same for Bassanio. Comment on these lines: 24–5, 73–4, 101–2, 183–5, 257–63, and 292–6

Follow-up

Now make a mood temperature graph for Bassanio for this scene.

1 Follow the pattern described on p. 102.
2 Decide which words should go at the top and bottom of the Y axis.
3 Plot the key moments for Bassanio in the scene.

Plot summary quiz

The 12 short quotations below sum up the story of this scene.

1 Work out the correct order for them.
2 Work out who said each one.

In a confrontation between Antonio and Shylock, Antonio soon gives up hope of pleading with him.

1 **look to him** keep a watch on him

2 **gratis** without charging interest

9 **naughty** worthless, useless

fond foolish

10 **abroad** out and about

14 **dull-eyed** easily deceived

16 **Christian intercessors** In the New Testament Christ is said to intercede, to plead with, God the Father for the salvation of sinful humans.

18 **impenetrable** assuming that it is impossible to get through to him

20 **bootless prayers** hopeless pleas

22–3 **I oft ... to me** I have often paid the bond due to him when his debtors appealed to me

Scene 3

Venice

Enter SHYLOCK, SOLANIO, ANTONIO, *and Gaoler*

SHYLOCK Gaoler, look to him, tell not me of mercy,
This is the fool that lent out money gratis.
Gaoler, look to him.

ANTONIO Hear me yet good Shylock.

SHYLOCK I'll have my bond, speak not against my bond,
I have sworn an oath that I will have my bond.
Thou call'dst me a dog before thou hadst a cause,
But since I am a dog beware my fangs.
The duke shall grant me justice. I do wonder,
Thou naughty gaoler, that thou art so fond
To come abroad with him at his request.

ANTONIO I pray thee hear me speak.

SHYLOCK I'll have my bond. I will not hear thee speak.
I'll have my bond, and therefore speak no more.
I'll not be made a soft and dull-eyed fool,
To shake the head, relent, and sigh, and yield
To Christian intercessors. Follow not;
I'll have no speaking. I will have my bond.

[*Exit*

SOLANIO It is the most impenetrable cur
That ever kept with men.

ANTONIO Let him alone,
I'll follow him no more with bootless prayers.
He seeks my life, his reason well I know;
I oft delivered from his forfeitures
Many that have at times made moan to me;
Therefore he hates me.

SOLANIO I am sure the duke
Will never grant this forfeiture to hold.

ANTONIO The duke cannot deny the course of law.

The forfeit is due the following day. Antonio hopes Bassanio will come to him.

27 **commodity** commercial privileges; Antonio understands that Venice, a city state whose wealth depends on trade with many nations, cannot afford to make exceptions to its law, or the whole basis of trust will be undermined.

29 **impeach** challenge, call into question

31 **Consisteth ... nations** is international

32 **bated** weakened

At Belmont, Lorenzo and Portia speak of Antonio and Bassanio.

2 **conceit** conception, understanding

3 **god-like amity** divine friendship

4 **bearing** putting up with

9 **Than ... you** than normal kindness could make you feel

12 **waste** spend

13 **egal yoke** equal share

14 **like** similar

15 **lineaments** distinctive characteristics

17 **bosom lover** close friend and confidant

18 **needs** of necessity

19–21 **How ... cruelty** how little is the amount I shall have spent in redeeming my husband's close friend from Shylock's devilish cruelty

For the commodity that strangers have
With us in Venice, if it be denied,
Will much impeach the justice of the state,
Since that the trade and profit of the city
Consisteth of all nations. Therefore go,
These griefs and losses have so bated me
That I shall hardly spare a pound of flesh
Tomorrow, to my bloody creditor.
Well, gaoler, on. Pray God Bassanio come
To see me pay his debt, and then I care not.

[*Exeunt*

Scene 4

Belmont

Enter PORTIA, NERISSA, LORENZO, JESSICA, *and* BALTHASAR

LORENZO
Madam, although I speak it in your presence,
You have a noble and a true conceit
Of god-like amity, which appears most strongly
In bearing thus the absence of your lord.
But if you knew to whom you show this honour,
How true a gentleman you send relief,
How dear a lover of my lord your husband,
I know you would be prouder of the work
Than customary bounty can enforce you.

PORTIA
I never did repent for doing good,
Nor shall not now. For in companions
That do converse and waste the time together,
Whose souls do bear an egal yoke of love,
There must be needs a like proportion
Of lineaments, of manners, and of spirit;
Which makes me think that this Antonio,
Being the bosom lover of my lord,
Must needs be like my lord. If it be so,
How little is the cost I have bestowed

Portia tells Lorenzo that she and Nerissa have promised to remain in prayer and contemplation until their husbands return. The house is in his care. She sends her servant on an errand to Padua.

25 **husbandry and manage** care and management

32 **abide** stay

33 **deny this imposition** refuse this task

37 **My people** i.e. her servants who run her household

38–9 **acknowledge … myself** accept you as temporary master and mistress of the house

48–9 **all ... speed** make as much haste as you can

52 **imagined speed** as quickly as possible

In purchasing the semblance of my soul
From out the state of hellish cruelty.
This comes too near the praising of myself,
Therefore no more of it; hear other things.
Lorenzo I commit into your hands
The husbandry and manage of my house,
Until my lord's return. For mine own part
I have toward heaven breathed a secret vow
To live in prayer and contemplation,
Only attended by Nerissa here,
Until her husband and my lord's return.
There is a monastery two miles off,
And there will we abide. I do desire you
Not to deny this imposition,
The which my love and some necessity
Now lays upon you.

LORENZO Madam, with all my heart,
I shall obey you in all fair commands.

PORTIA My people do already know my mind,
And will acknowledge you and Jessica
In place of Lord Bassanio and myself.
So fare you well till we shall meet again.

LORENZO Fair thoughts and happy hours attend on you.

JESSICA I wish your ladyship all heart's content.

PORTIA I thank you for your wish, and am well pleased
To wish it back on you. Fare you well Jessica.

[*Exeunt* JESSICA *and* LORENZO

Now Balthasar,
As I have ever found thee honest-true,
So let me find thee still. Take this same letter,
And use thou all the endeavour of a man
In speed to Padua. See thou render this
Into my cousin's hand, Doctor Bellario,
And look what notes and garments he doth give
thee,
Bring them I pray thee with imagined speed

Portia tells Nerissa that they are to dress as young men. She promises to tell her the rest of the plan when they are on their way in her coach.

53 **traject** crossing place, ferry

54 **trades** crosses over

59 **Before ... us** before they can expect to do so

60 **in such a habit** in such clothing, costume

61–2 **accomplished ... lack** equipped with what woman have not got

62 **wager** bet

63 **accoutred** dressed

65 **braver grace** more impressive elegance

66–7 **And speak ... voice** Portia is planning to disguise her voice by speaking like a young man whose voice is breaking.

68–9 **speak ... youth** she will boast of fights

69 **quaint** cleverly conceived, invented

72 **I ... withal** I could not help it

77 **raw** immature

bragging Jacks boasting fellows

79 **turn to** become

81 **If ... interpreter** you wouldn't want someone to misinterpret that in an unpleasant way

82 **device** scheme

83 **stays** will wait

Unto the traject, to the common ferry
Which trades to Venice. Waste no time in words
But get thee gone. I shall be there before thee.

BALTHASAR Madam, I go with all convenient speed.

[*Exit*

PORTIA Come on Nerissa, I have work in hand
That you yet know not of; we'll see our husbands
Before they think of us.

NERISSA Shall they see us?

PORTIA They shall Nerissa; but in such a habit
That they shall think we are accomplished
With that we lack. I'll hold thee any wager,
When we are both accoutred like young men,
I'll prove the prettier fellow of the two,
And wear my dagger with the braver grace,
And speak between the change of man and boy
With a reed voice, and turn two mincing steps
Into a manly stride, and speak of frays
Like a fine bragging youth; and tell quaint lies
How honourable ladies sought my love,
Which I denying, they fell sick and died –
I could not do withal. Then I'll repent,
And wish for all that, that I had not killed them;
And twenty of these puny lies I'll tell,
That men shall swear I've discontinued school
Above a twelvemonth. I have within my mind
A thousand raw tricks of these bragging Jacks
Which I will practise.

NERISSA Why, shall we turn to men?

PORTIA Fie, what a question's that,
If thou wert near a lewd interpreter.
But come, I'll tell thee all my whole device
When I am in my coach, which stays for us
At the park gate; and therefore haste away,
For we must measure twenty miles today.

[*Exeunt*

At Belmont, Launcelot is jokingly assuring Jessica that she has no hope of going to heaven. Lorenzo joins them.

1 **sins ... father** Launcelot has half remembered a statement from the Old Testament.

2–3 **I fear you** I fear for you

4 **agitation** the thoughts that have been bothering me

7 **bastard** 1) illegitimate 2) without any sound basis

9–10 **hope ... you not** hope that Shylock is not your real father

11 **bastard hope** Jessica takes up the word 'bastard'. If she has a different father then her mother has sinned.

14–15 **Thus ... mother** Launcelot now jokes about the difficulty Jessica is in. Scylla was a dangerous rock, home to a monster, and Charybdis a fierce whirlpool. They were situated opposite one another in the Straits of Messina and sailors had to try to steer between them.

17–18 **I shall ... Christian** Jessica claims she will be saved because in marrying Lorenzo she became a Christian

20 **enow** enough

22–4 **if we ... money** any more Christians (who, unlike Jews, are pork-eaters) will raise the price of pigs and there will be shortages

Scene 5

Belmont

Enter LAUNCELOT *and* JESSICA

LAUNCELOT Yes truly; for look you, the sins of the father are to be laid upon the children, therefore I promise ye, I fear you. I was always plain with you, and so now I speak my agitation of the matter. Therefore be of good cheer, for truly I think you are damned. There is but one hope in it that can do you any good, and that is but a kind of bastard hope neither.

JESSICA And what hope is that I pray thee?

LAUNCELOT Marry you may partly hope that your father got you not, that you are not the Jew's daughter.

JESSICA That were a kind of bastard hope indeed, so the sins of my mother should be visited upon me.

LAUNCELOT Truly then I fear you are damned both by father and mother. Thus when I shun Scylla your father, I fall into Charybdis your mother; well, you are gone both ways.

JESSICA I shall be saved by my husband, he hath made me a Christian.

LAUNCELOT Truly the more to blame he, we were Christians enow before, e'en as many as could well live one by another. This making of Christians will raise the price of hogs: if we grow all to be pork-eaters, we shall not shortly have a rasher on the coals for money.

Enter LORENZO

JESSICA I'll tell my husband, Launcelot, what you say. Here he comes.

LORENZO I shall grow jealous of you shortly Launcelot, if you

Lorenzo tells Launcelot to order dinner. This produces more witty nonsense from him. Lorenzo and Jessica are at last alone.

28 **corners** out of the way, secluded places

30 **out** no longer getting on with each other

35 **the ... wit** the most elegant form of wit

36–7 **discourse ... parrots** the only proper conversation will be between parrots

39 **stomachs** appetites

40 **wit-snapper** clever-dick

42 **'cover'** Launcelot is insisting on the proper word for laying the table, as dinner is already prepared.

45 **Yet ... occasion** Lorenzo is exasperated with Launcelot's continual playing about with words.

52 **humours and conceits** moods and fancies

54 **O ... suited** O such good sense, how he can adapt his words

58 **Garnished** dressed

58–9 **for a ... matter** with cleverly playful words that don't get the sense across

59 **How cheer'st thou** How are things with you

thus get my wife into corners.

JESSICA Nay, you need not fear us Lorenzo. Launcelot and I are out. He tells me flatly there is no mercy for me in heaven, because I am a Jew's daughter. And he says you are no good member of the commonwealth, for in converting Jews to Christians, you raise the price of pork.

LORENZO I think the best grace of wit will shortly turn into silence, and discourse grow commendable in none only but parrots. Go in sirrah, bid them prepare for dinner.

LAUNCELOT That is done sir, they have all stomachs.

LORENZO Goodly Lord, what a wit-snapper are you. Then bid them prepare dinner.

LAUNCELOT That is done too sir, only 'cover' is the word.

LORENZO Will you cover then sir?

LAUNCELOT Not so sir neither, I know my duty.

LORENZO Yet more quarrelling with occasion. Wilt thou show the whole wealth of thy wit in an instant? I pray thee understand a plain man in his plain meaning. Go to thy fellows, bid them cover the table, serve in the meat, and we will come in to dinner.

LAUNCELOT For the table sir, it shall be served in, for the meat sir, it shall be covered, for your coming in to dinner sir, why let it be as humours and conceits shall govern.

[*Exit*

LORENZO O dear discretion, how his words are suited.
The fool hath planted in his memory
An army of good words, and I do know
A many fools that stand in better place,
Garnished like him, that for a tricksy word
Defy the matter. How cheer'st thou Jessica?
And now good sweet, say thy opinion,
How dost thou like the Lord Bassanio's wife?

Jessica is very impressed with Portia. Lorenzo playfully tries to turn some of this praise on to himself.

62 **Past all expressing** Beyond my power to say

It is very meet It is very fitting

63 **live** should live

66–7 **And if ... heaven** if he didn't deserve these joys while on earth then he certainly shouldn't go to heaven when he dies

68–9 **if two ... women** if two gods were to lay a bet on two women on earth

70–1 **there ... other** there would have to be something added to the other who's not Portia to even things up

71 **rude** harsh

72 **her fellow** her equal

76 **let ... stomach** let me praise you while I feel like it

JESSICA
Past all expressing. It is very meet
The Lord Bassanio live an upright life,
For having such a blessing in his lady,
He finds the joys of heaven here on earth,
And if on earth he do not merit it,
In reason he should never come to heaven.
Why, if two gods should play some heavenly
  match,
And on the wager lay two earthly women,
And Portia one, there must be something else
Pawned with the other, for the poor rude world
Hath not her fellow.

LORENZO
Even such a husband
Hast thou of me, as she is for a wife.

JESSICA
Nay, but ask my opinion too of that.

LORENZO
I will anon, first let us go to dinner.

JESSICA
Nay, let me praise you while I have a stomach.

LORENZO
No pray thee, let it serve for table-talk,
Then howsoe'er thou speak'st, 'mong other things
I shall digest it.

JESSICA
Well, I'll set you forth.

[*Exeunt*

Act 3 scenes 3 to 5

Character: Antonio

In Act 3 scene 3 we watch Antonio as his last hopes for mercy are dashed by Shylock. The scene adds to our understanding of Antonio's character.

Work with a partner

1 Make a list of at least four words that describe Antonio's behaviour in this scene. You can choose from the list and/or use words of your own.

Warning: the list contains some words that are *not* suitable to describe Antonio.

puzzled	angry	depressed	pleading
intelligent	patient	thoughtful	resigned
understanding	argumentative	sad	passive

2 For each of the words you have chosen, find some evidence to support your choice. Copy the table below and use it to record your ideas. (You should add four more words to the table.)

3 Use the 'Explanation' column to link the word you have chosen and the evidence you have found.

Word	Evidence	Explanation
pleading	'I pray thee hear me speak'	He is begging Shylock to listen to what he has to say.

The other side of the coin

Scene 3 shows one side of Antonio's character, but it is not the only one.

1 Look back at Act 1 scene 3 and read lines 103–34 again.

2 Make a similar table, this time choosing four words of your own.

3 Use your two tables to prepare a short presentation for the rest of the class, entitled, 'Two sides of Antonio's character'.

Performance: Portia

In Act 3 scene 4, Portia drops a bombshell: she is going to dress up as a man and travel to Venice, but she doesn't explain why.

Work with a partner

1 On your own, each read lines 60–78, in which Portia describes how she will behave as a man.

2 Take a piece of paper and make a list of words and phrases that give us clues about how she will behave as a 'man', for example:

> 1. change the way she speaks
> 2. walk

3 Think about how she could show each of these things as she speaks the words. For example, she could 'speak with a reed voice' (line 67) for that part of the speech. Add these ideas to your list, for example:

> 1. change the way she speaks – 'speak with a reed voice'
> 2. walk

4 Now try acting out the speech. One of you is the actor playing the part of Portia, and the other is the director.

5 Now swap over and try the speech again.

6 Compare the two versions and discuss how to combine the best bits from each. Work on a version to present to the rest of the class.

What about Nerissa?

At the beginning of scene 3 Portia is the only person who knows about her plans. So what does Nerissa make of all this?

1 Make a list of words and phrases to describe how Nerissa acts – and reacts – at each of these points in the scene:

a lines 24–32

b lines 45–55

c lines 60–3

Getting graphic

You may have seen graphic adaptations of a Shakespeare play. Examples are: *Manga Shakespeare* and *Page Becomes the Stage*. Sometimes these books use the whole text, and sometimes they cut the text down.

Work with a partner

1 You are going to design and create two pages for a graphic Shakespeare book.

2 Choose one of these scenes:
- Act 3 scene 3 (all)
- Act 3 scene 4 (lines 24–69)

3 Discuss what are the main frames you want on each page. Remember that:
- frames can be of different sizes – you can even devote a whole page to a single picture
- frames can be different shapes – they don't all have to be rectangles.

4 Discuss what each character should look like and what the setting looks like.

5 Make a rough diagram and write in each frame what it will contain using:
- a short description of the picture
- the words to go in the speech bubbles, (remember that you can cut the text), for example:

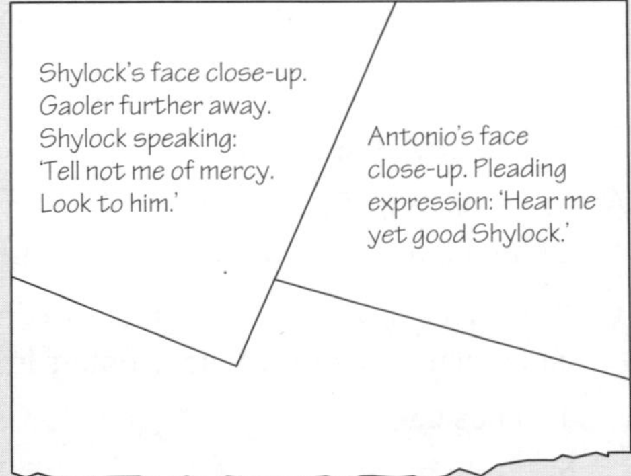

6 Now take one page each. Use a large sheet of paper and draw up your final page.

Quotation quiz

For each of these quotations, work out:

1 who said it
2 who they were speaking to
3 what it tells us about:
   a the speaker
   b the situation
   c any other characters.

I never did repent for doing good,
Nor shall not now.
A

See thou render this
Into my cousin's hand,
Doctor Bellario...
B

Therefore be of good cheer,
for truly I think you are damned.
C

The fool hath planted
in his memory
An army of good words...
D

There is a monastery
two miles off,
And there will we abide.
E

Thou call'dst me dog before thou
hadst a cause,
But since I am a dog beware my fangs.
F

Pray God Bassanio come
To see me pay his debt, and
then I care not.
G

I oft delivered from his forfeitures
Many that have at times made
moan to me...
H

I'll have my bond,
and therefore speak
no more.
I

I'll prove the prettier fellow of the two,
And wear my dagger with the braver grace...
J

The Duke arrives to preside over the decision to be made about the payment of Antonio's bond. He expresses sympathy with Antonio and assumes that Shylock will relent at last.

6 **dram** drop

7 **ta'en** taken

qualify moderate

10 **Out of ... reach** out of reach of his malice

18 **fashion** pretence

19 **last ... act** the eleventh hour

20 **remorse** compassion

strange remarkable

22 **where ... penalty** whereas you now say you want to exact the penalty

Act Four

Scene 1

Venice

Enter the DUKE, *the magnificoes,* ANTONIO, BASSANIO, GRATIANO, SALERIO, *and others*

DUKE What, is Antonio here?

ANTONIO Ready, so please your grace.

DUKE I am sorry for thee, thou art come to answer
A stony adversary, an inhuman wretch,
Uncapable of pity, void and empty
From any dram of mercy.

ANTONIO I have heard
Your grace hath ta'en great pains to qualify
His rigorous course; but since he stands obdurate,
And that no lawful means can carry me
Out of his envy's reach, I do oppose
My patience to his fury, and am armed
To suffer with a quietness of spirit,
The very tyranny and rage of his.

DUKE Go one and call the Jew into the court.

SALERIO He is ready at the door, he comes my lord.

Enter SHYLOCK

DUKE Make room, and let him stand before our face.
Shylock, the world thinks, and I think so too,
That thou but lead'st this fashion of thy malice
To the last hour of act, and then 'tis thought
Thou'lt show thy mercy and remorse more strange
Than is thy strange apparent cruelty;
And where thou now exacts the penalty,

The Duke tells Shylock that they are expecting him to be generous. Shylock replies that he has said what he intends to do, he has sworn it, and he will do it, purely because it suits him to do so – he hates Antonio.

24 **loose the forfeiture** give up claim to the forfeit (the pound of flesh)

26 **moiety ... principal** portion of the original sum loaned

29 **Enow** enough

30–2 **pluck ... Tartars** The Duke suggests that Antonio's heavy losses have been so overwhelming that they should extract pity from the most hard-hearted.

Turks, and Tartars (notorious for cruel and barbaric behaviour)

33 **offices ... courtesy** acts of civilised behaviour

35 **possessed** informed

purpose intend to do

38 **let ... light** then let the damage be done

43 **humour** whim, fancy

46 **baned** poisoned

47 **gaping pig** boar's head (a dish served at table); the mouth would be open with an apple inside it. A Jew could well be offended by this.

49 **sings i' the nose** makes a noise like someone singing through their nose

50 **affection** emotion

51 **passion** strong feeling

53 **rendered** given

56–7 **but ... shame** the man who passes water in public (because that's what the sound of a bagpipe makes him do – see line 50) cannot help himself, although he is ashamed

60 **lodged hate** settled, abiding hatred

Which is a pound of this poor merchant's flesh,
Thou wilt not only loose the forfeiture,
But touched with human gentleness and love,
Forgive a moiety of the principal,
Glancing an eye of pity on his losses
That have of late so huddled on his back,
Enow to press a royal merchant down,
And pluck commiseration of his state
From brassy bosoms and rough hearts of flint,
From stubborn Turks, and Tartars never trained
To offices of tender courtesy.
We all expect a gentle answer Jew.

SHYLOCK I have possessed your grace of what I purpose;
And by our holy Sabbath have I sworn
To have the due and forfeit of my bond.
If you deny it, let the danger light
Upon your charter and your city's freedom.
You'll ask me why I rather choose to have
A weight of carrion flesh, than to receive
Three thousand ducats. I'll not answer that,
But say it is my humour; is it answered?
What if my house be troubled with a rat,
And I be pleased to give ten thousand ducats
To have it baned? What, are you answered yet?
Some men there are love not a gaping pig;
Some that are mad if they behold a cat;
And others, when the bagpipe sings i' the nose,
Cannot contain their urine; for affection,
Master of passion, sways it to the mood
Of what it likes or loathes. Now for your answer:
As there is no firm reason to be rendered
Why he cannot abide a gaping pig;
Why he, a harmless necessary cat;
Why he, a woollen bagpipe; but of force
Must yield to such inevitable shame,
As to offend, himself being offended;
So can I give no reason, nor I will not,
More than a lodged hate and a certain loathing

Bassanio argues with Shylock. Antonio knows there is no point in this. Bassanio offers twice the loan. Shylock refuses. He insists on having what he has 'bought'.

62 **losing suit** Winning the case will cost Shylock the money.

70 **think** bear in mind

72 **main flood** high tide

bate reduce

77 **fretten** buffeted

81 **moe** more

farther means other methods

82 **with ... conveniency** with simple proceedings and all decent speed

87 **draw** accept

92 **in abject ... parts** in miserable and servile tasks

I bear Antonio, that I follow thus
A losing suit against him. Are you answered?

BASSANIO This is no answer thou unfeeling man,
To excuse the current of thy cruelty.

SHYLOCK I am not bound to please thee with my answers.

BASSANIO Do all men kill the things they do not love?

SHYLOCK Hates any man the thing he would not kill?

BASSANIO Every offence is not a hate at first.

SHYLOCK What, wouldst thou have a serpent sting thee twice?

ANTONIO I pray you think you question with the Jew.
You may as well go stand upon the beach
And bid the main flood bate his usual height;
You may as well use question with the wolf
Why he hath made the ewe bleat for the lamb;
You may as well forbid the mountain pines
To wag their high tops and to make no noise
When they are fretten with the gusts of heaven;
You may as well do anything most hard
As seek to soften that – than which what's harder? –
His Jewish heart. Therefore I do beseech you
Make no moe offers, use no farther means,
But with all brief and plain conveniency
Let me have judgement, and the Jew his will.

BASSANIO For thy three thousand ducats, here is six.

SHYLOCK If every ducat in six thousand ducats
Were in six parts, and every part a ducat,
I would not draw them, I would have my bond.

DUKE How shalt thou hope for mercy, rendering none?

SHYLOCK What judgement shall I dread, doing no wrong?
You have among you many a purchased slave,
Which, like your asses, and your dogs and mules,
You use in abject and in slavish parts,
Because you bought them. Shall I say to you,
'Let them be free, marry them to your heirs?

Shylock suggests that the law of Venice will be worthless if he cannot have judgement. Bassanio sees hope in the arrival of a messenger from Padua. Nerissa presents a letter while Shylock sharpens his knife on the sole of his shoe.

96–7 **let ... with** let their tastebuds enjoy

97 **viands** food

104 **Upon my power** By my authority

106 **determine** decide, judge

107 **stays without** is waiting outside

109 **new come** just arrived

114 **tainted wether** sick ram (a **metaphor** (see Glossary p. 241) – 'wether' often means a castrated ram)

115 **Meetest for death** best killed

118 **live still** go on living

epitaph inscription on a gravestone

121 **whet** sharpen

125–6 **bear ... envy** be made half as cutting as your sharp hatred

Why sweat they under burdens? Let their beds
Be made as soft as yours, and let their palates
Be seasoned with such viands. You will answer,
'The slaves are ours'; so do I answer you.
The pound of flesh which I demand of him
Is dearly bought, 'tis mine and I will have it.
If you deny me, fie upon your law,
There is no force in the decrees of Venice.
I stand for judgement. Answer: shall I have it?

DUKE Upon my power I may dismiss this court,
Unless Bellario a learned doctor,
Whom I have sent for to determine this,
Come here today.

SALERIO My lord, here stays without
A messenger with letters from the doctor,
New come from Padua.

DUKE Bring us the letters. Call the messenger.

BASSANIO Good cheer Antonio. What man, courage yet.
The Jew shall have my flesh, blood, bones and all,
Ere thou shalt lose for me one drop of blood.

ANTONIO I am a tainted wether of the flock,
Meetest for death. The weakest kind of fruit
Drops earliest to the ground, and so let me.
You cannot better be employed Bassanio,
Than to live still and write mine epitaph.

Enter NERISSA, *dressed like a lawyer's clerk*

DUKE Came you from Padua, from Bellario?

NERISSA From both, my lord. Bellario greets your grace.
[*Presents a letter*

BASSANIO Why dost thou whet thy knife so earnestly?

SHYLOCK To cut the forfeiture from that bankrupt there.

GRATIANO Not on thy sole, but on thy soul, harsh Jew,
Thou mak'st thy knife keen. But no metal can,
No, not the hangman's axe, bear half the keenness

Gratiano now tries insults but Shylock insists he will have his legal rights. The letter from Bellario introduces Balthasar a young lawyer, in fact Portia, accompanied by Nerissa, both in disguise.

126 **pierce** get through to

127 **wit** intelligence

128 **inexecrable** most accursed

129 **for ... accused** justice is at fault, seeing that you are still alive

130 **my faith** i.e. the faith of a Christian

131 **hold opinion** agree

Pythagoras the Greek philosopher and mathematician; he believed in the transmigration of souls – the idea that in a process of purification (or punishment) a person's soul on their death can enter the body of another person or an animal, and an animal's soul can enter another animal or a person.

132 **infuse** pour, instil

133 **trunks** bodies

currish quarrelsome

134 **Governed a wolf** was controlled by a wolf

135 **fell** deadly

fleet pass away (from his body)

136 **whilst ... dam** while you still lay inside your pagan mother's womb

139 **Till ... bond** Until you can get the seal off my bond by complaining so bitterly

140 **Thou but offendest** you're only damaging

141 **wit** intellect

142 **cureless** incurable

152–3 **in loving visitation** on a friendly visit

156 **we ... together** together we consulted many books for similar cases

156–7 **he ... opinion** he has been provided with my opinion on the case

160 **importunity** request

Of thy sharp envy. Can no prayers pierce thee?

SHYLOCK No, none that thou hast wit enough to make.

GRATIANO O, be thou damned, inexecrable dog,
And for thy life let justice be accused.
Thou almost mak'st me waver in my faith,
To hold opinion with Pythagoras,
That souls of animals infuse themselves
Into the trunks of men. Thy currish spirit
Governed a wolf, who hanged for human slaughter,
Even from the gallows did his fell soul fleet,
And whilst thou layest in thy unhallowed dam,
Infused itself in thee; for thy desires
Are wolvish, bloody, starved, and ravenous.

SHYLOCK Till thou canst rail the seal from off my bond,
Thou but offendest thy lungs to speak so loud.
Repair thy wit good youth, or it will fall
To cureless ruin. I stand here for law.

DUKE This letter from Bellario doth commend
A young and learned doctor to our court.
Where is he?

NERISSA He attendeth here hard by
To know your answer whether you'll admit him.

DUKE With all my heart. Some three or four of you
Go give him courteous conduct to this place.
Meantime the court shall hear Bellario's letter.

CLERK [*Reads*] 'Your Grace shall understand that at the receipt of your letter I am very sick, but in the instant that your messenger came, in loving visitation was with me a young doctor of Rome; his name is Balthasar. I acquainted him with the cause in controversy between the Jew and Antonio the merchant; we turned o'er many books together; he is furnished with my opinion, which bettered with his own learning, the greatness whereof I cannot enough commend, comes with him at my importunity, to fill up your Grace's request in

Once the letter has been read, Portia is admitted to the court as Bellario's young acquaintance, Balthasar, and meets the protagonists. She too suggests Shylock should show mercy, and gives her definition of the word.

161 **my stead** in place of me; the audience knows that the 'young doctor' of Bellario's letter is Portia. She is accompanied by Nerissa as her clerk. Because the audience knows what the characters on stage do not know this is called **dramatic irony** (see Glossary p. 239).

161–2 **let ... impediment** do not let his youth stand in the way of granting him serious consideration

165 **whose ... commendation** his conduct will be a better recommendation than any words of mine

170 **the difference** the dispute

172 **throughly** thoroughly

176 **suit you follow** the case you are involved in

177 **in such rule** so correctly presented

178 **impugn you** oppose you (in law)

179 **You ... danger** you are at risk from him

181 **Then ... merciful** The Jew has to show mercy

183 **quality** nature

is not strained cannot be forced

187 **becomes** suits

my stead. I beseech you let his lack of years be no impediment to let him lack a reverend estimation, for I never knew so young a body with so old a head. I leave him to your gracious acceptance, whose trial shall better publish his commendation.'

DUKE You hear the learned Bellario what he writes,
And here, I take it, is the doctor come.

Enter PORTIA, *dressed like a doctor of laws*

Give me your hand. Came you from old Bellario?

PORTIA I did my lord.

DUKE You are welcome, take your place.
Are you acquainted with the difference
That holds this present question in the court?

PORTIA I am informed throughly of the cause.
Which is the merchant here? And which the Jew?

DUKE Antonio and old Shylock, both stand forth.

PORTIA Is your name Shylock?

SHYLOCK Shylock is my name.

PORTIA Of a strange nature is the suit you follow,
Yet in such rule that the Venetian law
Cannot impugn you as you do proceed.
You stand within his danger, do you not?

ANTONIO Ay, so he says.

PORTIA Do you confess the bond?

ANTONIO I do.

PORTIA Then must the Jew be merciful.

SHYLOCK On what compulsion must I? Tell me that.

PORTIA The quality of mercy is not strained,
It droppeth as the gentle rain from heaven
Upon the place beneath. It is twice blest,
It blesseth him that gives, and him that takes.
'Tis mightiest in the mightiest, it becomes
The throned monarch better than his crown.

Portia continues with her definition of mercy. Shylock still demands 'justice' and refuses Bassanio's offers of money and self-sacrifice. As Portia upholds the law, Shylock is jubilant.

189 **temporal** worldly (as opposed to religious)

190 **attribute to** symbol of

192 **sceptred sway** temporal rule

194 **attribute to** quality, characteristic of

196 **seasons** moderates

198 **in ... justice** if there were true justice (i.e. that of God)

200 **And ... prayer** i.e. the Lord's Prayer

202 **mitigate** reduce the severity of

205 **My ... head** Shylock takes full responsibility for his actions

207 **discharge** pay

208 **tender** offer

213 **malice ... truth** evil intent overwhelms righteousness

214 **Wrest ... authority** Bassanio is suggesting that just this once the doctor could use his authority to give the law a slightly more liberal interpretation.

216 **curb** check, frustrate

of his will from getting what he wants

219 **precedent** an example of a judgement on which later cases may then be based

222 **Daniel** A reference to the story of Susannah in the Apocrypha; she was accused of immoral behaviour by two elders, whose advances she had rejected. He questioned them separately and was able to prove they were lying. They were put to death.

His sceptre shows the force of temporal power,
The attribute to awe and majesty,
Wherein doth sit the dread and fear of kings.
But mercy is above this sceptred sway,
It is enthroned in the hearts of kings,
It is an attribute to God himself;
And earthly power doth then show likest God's
When mercy seasons justice. Therefore Jew,
Though justice be thy plea, consider this,
That in the course of justice, none of us
Should see salvation. We do pray for mercy,
And that same prayer doth teach us all to render
The deeds of mercy. I have spoke thus much
To mitigate the justice of thy plea,
Which, if thou follow, this strict court of Venice
Must needs give sentence 'gainst the merchant there.

SHYLOCK My deeds upon my head, I crave the law,
The penalty and forfeit of my bond.

PORTIA Is he not able to discharge the money?

BASSANIO Yes, here I tender it for him in the court,
Yea, twice the sum, if that will not suffice,
I will be bound to pay it ten times o'er
On forfeit of my hands, my head, my heart.
If this will not suffice, it must appear
That malice bears down truth. And I beseech you
Wrest once the law to your authority:
To do a great right, do a little wrong,
And curb this cruel devil of his will.

PORTIA It must not be, there is no power in Venice
Can alter a decree establishèd.
'Twill be recorded for a precedent,
And many an error by the same example
Will rush into the state. It cannot be.

SHYLOCK A Daniel come to judgement. Yea a Daniel.
O wise young judge, how I do honour thee.

PORTIA I pray you let me look upon the bond.

Although Portia mentions three times the sum and asks for mercy, Shylock cannot be moved. The bond must stand and Antonio must get ready to have a pound of flesh cut away.

228 **perjury** usually refers to the telling of a lie when a person has sworn to tell the truth. Here the suggestion is that Shylock will not go back on the oath he apparently took in the synagogue, witnessed by Tubal, to take vengeance on Antonio (Act 3 scene 1 line 124).

234 **tenor** the actual wording of a legal document

236 **exposition** explanation, setting out of the facts

238 **Whereof ... pillar** of which you deserve to be seen as a strong supporter (A 'pillar of society' is a well-known member of society, who upholds its values.)

240–1 **no ... me** no one can persuade me to change my mind

241 **stay** make my stand

246 **intent** meaning

254 **Are there balance** Is there a pair of scales

SHYLOCK Here 'tis, most reverend doctor, here it is.

PORTIA Shylock there's thrice thy money offered thee.

SHYLOCK An oath, an oath, I have an oath in heaven.
Shall I lay perjury upon my soul?
No, not for Venice.

PORTIA Why this bond is forfeit,
And lawfully by this the Jew may claim
A pound of flesh, to be by him cut off
Nearest the merchant's heart. Be merciful,
Take thrice thy money, bid me tear the bond.

SHYLOCK When it is paid according to the tenor.
It doth appear you are a worthy judge;
You know the law, your exposition
Hath been most sound. I charge you by the law,
Whereof you are a well-deserving pillar,
Proceed to judgement. By my soul I swear
There is no power in the tongue of man
To alter me, I stay here on my bond.

ANTONIO Most heartily I do beseech the court
To give the judgement.

PORTIA Why then thus it is:
You must prepare your bosom for his knife.

SHYLOCK O noble judge, O excellent young man.

PORTIA For the intent and purpose of the law
Hath full relation to the penalty,
Which here appeareth due upon the bond.

SHYLOCK 'Tis very true. O wise and upright judge,
How much more elder art thou than thy looks.

PORTIA Therefore lay bare your bosom.

SHYLOCK Ay, his breast,
So says the bond, doth it not noble judge?
'Nearest his heart', those are the very words.

PORTIA It is so. Are there balance here to weigh
The flesh?

Portia expects there to be a surgeon present, at Shylock's expense, to prevent Antonio from bleeding to death. Antonio gives what he thinks has to be his last speech. Bassanio declares he would sacrifice his wife and everything else for Antonio's life. Gratiano joins in.

256 **on your charge** at your expense

258 **Is ... nominated** Does it say so

263 **armed** resolved, settled in my mind

267 **use** habit, practice

273 **the process ... end** how Antonio met his end (with a **play on words** (see Glossary p. 242), since 'process' can mean 'trial')

274 **speak me fair** speak well of me

277–8 **Repent/repents** Regret/regrets

280 **with all my heart** He means emotionally and literally, making a brave joke just before his death.

284 **esteemed** valued

SHYLOCK I have them ready.

PORTIA Have by some surgeon Shylock, on your charge,
To stop his wounds, lest he do bleed to death.

SHYLOCK Is it so nominated in the bond?

PORTIA It is not so expressed, but what of that?
'Twere good you do so much for charity.

SHYLOCK I cannot find it, 'tis not in the bond.

PORTIA You merchant, have you anything to say?

ANTONIO But little; I am armed and well prepared.
Give me your hand Bassanio, fare you well.
Grieve not that I am fallen to this for you;
For herein Fortune shows herself more kind
Than is her custom: it is still her use
To let the wretched man outlive this wealth,
To view with hollow eye and wrinkled brow
An age of poverty; from which lingering penance
Of such misery doth she cut me off.
Commend me to your honourable wife.
Tell her the process of Antonio's end.
Say how I loved you, speak me fair in death;
And when the tale is told, bid her be judge
Whether Bassanio had not once a love.
Repent but you that you shall lose your friend,
And he repents not that he pays your debt.
For if the Jew do cut but deep enough,
I'll pay it presently with all my heart.

BASSANIO Antonio, I am married to a wife
Which is as dear to me as life itself,
But life itself, my wife, and all the world,
Are not with me esteemed above thy life.
I would lose all, ay sacrifice them all
Here to this devil, to deliver you.

PORTIA Your wife would give you little thanks for that,
If she were by to hear you make the offer.

GRATIANO I have a wife whom I protest I love,

Portia declares the law says Shylock may take his pound of flesh – but no blood. Shylock tries now to settle for the offer of nine thousand ducats.

291 **Entreat** beg for

currish dog-like

293 **else** otherwise

295 **Barrabas** The thief (a Jew) whom the crowd asked Pontius Pilate to release instead of Jesus.

297 **trifle** waste

304 **Tarry** Wait

305 **no jot of blood** not the tiniest amount of blood

310–11 **confiscate Unto** to be seized by

314 **urgest** press for, demand

I would she were in heaven, so she could
Entreat some power to change this currish Jew.

NERISSA 'Tis well you offer it behind her back,
The wish would make else an unquiet house.

SHYLOCK [*Aside*] These be the Christian husbands. I have a daughter –
Would any of the stock of Barrabas
Had been her husband rather than a Christian.
[*Aloud*] We trifle time, I pray thee pursue sentence.

PORTIA A pound of that same merchant's flesh is thine;
The court awards it, and the law doth give it.

SHYLOCK Most rightful judge.

PORTIA And you must cut this flesh from off his breast;
The law allows it, and the court awards it.

SHYLOCK Most learned judge. A sentence. Come prepare.

PORTIA Tarry a little, there is something else.
This bond doth give thee here no jot of blood,
The words expressly are 'a pound of flesh'.
Take then thy bond, take thou thy pound of flesh,
But in the cutting it, if thou doth shed
One drop of Christian blood, thy lands and goods
Are by the laws of Venice confiscate
Unto the state of Venice.

GRATIANO O upright judge – mark, Jew – O learned judge.

SHYLOCK Is that the law?

PORTIA Thyself shalt see the act.
For as thou urgest justice, be assured
Thou shalt have justice more than thou desirest.

GRATIANO O upright judge – mark, Jew – a learned judge.

SHYLOCK I take this offer then. Pay the bond thrice
And let the Christian go.

BASSANIO Here is the money.

Portia announces the penalty if Shylock takes more or less than his bond. Gratiano gloats. Shylock has now lost even the original loan. He wants to leave but there is now a case against him.

319 **Soft** Wait

320 **all justice** everything the law provides for

soft, no haste just a moment, there's no hurry

327 **substance** amount

329 **scruple** measure equal to about 1 gram (so one twentieth part would be about 0.05 gm)

333 **I have ... hip** Gratiano has Shylock at a disadvantage. (See note on Act 1 scene 3 line 43.)

343 **at thy peril** at your own risk

345 **Tarry** Wait

348 **alien** non-Venetian

350 **seek the life** tries to kill

351 **contrive** plot

PORTIA Soft.
The Jew shall have all justice – soft, no haste –
He shall have nothing but the penalty.

GRATIANO O Jew, an upright judge, a learned judge.

PORTIA Therefore prepare thee to cut off the flesh.
Shed thou no blood, nor cut thou less nor more
But just a pound of flesh. If thou tak'st more
Or less than a just pound, be it but so much
As makes it light or heavy in the substance,
Or the division of the twentieth part
Of one poor scruple – nay, if the scale do turn
But in the estimation of a hair,
Thou diest, and all thy goods are confiscate.

GRATIANO A second Daniel, a Daniel, Jew.
Now, infidel, I have you on the hip.

PORTIA Why doth the Jew pause? Take thy forfeiture.

SHYLOCK Give me my principal, and let me go.

BASSANIO I have it ready for thee, here it is.

PORTIA He hath refused it in the open court.
He shall have merely justice and his bond.

GRATIANO A Daniel still say I, a second Daniel.
I thank thee Jew for teaching me that word.

SHYLOCK Shall I not have barely my principal?

PORTIA Thou shalt have nothing but the forfeiture
To be so taken at thy peril Jew.

SHYLOCK Why then the devil give him good of it.
I'll stay no longer question.

PORTIA Tarry Jew.
The law hath yet another hold on you.
It is enacted in the laws of Venice,
If it be proved against an alien
That by direct, or indirect attempts
He seek the life of any citizen,
The party 'gainst the which he doth contrive
Shall seize one half his goods, the other half

The tables have been turned on Shylock. He is in danger of death or ruin. Portia asks Antonio what mercy he can grant. He is concerned to help Lorenzo and Jessica.

353 **privy ... state** the treasury that belongs entirely and only to the state

355 **'gainst ... voice** and no one can do anything about it

357 **manifest proceeding** quite obvious actions

361 **formerly ... rehearsed** mentioned by me earlier

364–5 **yet ... cord** because all your possessions now belong to the state you cannot even afford a length of rope

367 **spirit** attitude

371 **humbleness ... fine** a sufficiently humble attitude may allow us to reduce it to a fine

372 **Ay ... Antonio** The state's share can be reduced to a fine, but not Antonio's

374 **house** 'House' means both 'dwelling' and 'family' with a memory of ancestors and a consciousness of descendants to come, all belonging to it.

378 **A halter gratis** A noose for free

380 **to quit the fine** to do away with the fine

381 **so** provided that

382 **in use** in trust

382–4 **to render ... daughter** so that Lorenzo will inherit it on Shylock's death

Comes to the privy coffer of the state,
And the offender's life lies in the mercy
Of the duke only, 'gainst all other voice.
In which predicament I say thou stand'st;
For it appears by manifest proceeding,
That indirectly, and directly too,
Thou hast contrived against the very life
Of the defendant; and thou hast incurred
The danger formerly by me rehearsed.
Down therefore, and beg mercy of the duke.

GRATIANO Beg that thou mayst have leave to hang thyself.
And yet thy wealth being forfeit to the state,
Thou hast not left the value of a cord,
Therefore thou must be hanged at the state's charge.

DUKE That thou shalt see the difference of our spirit,
I pardon thee thy life before thou ask it.
For half thy wealth, it is Antonio's,
The other half comes to the general state,
Which humbleness may drive unto a fine.

PORTIA Ay, for the state, not for Antonio.

SHYLOCK Nay, take my life and all, pardon not that.
You take my house, when you do take the prop
That doth sustain my house; you take my life,
When you do take the means whereby I live.

PORTIA What mercy can you render him Antonio?

GRATIANO A halter gratis – nothing else, for God's sake.

ANTONIO So please my lord the duke and all the court
To quit the fine for one half of his goods,
I am content – so he will let me have
The other half in use – to render it
Upon his death unto the gentleman
That lately stole his daughter.
Two things provided more, that for this favour,
He presently become a Christian;

Shylock is forced to provide for his daughter and Lorenzo. He claims he feels ill and is given leave to go. Portia refuses the Duke's invitation to dinner. She receives Bassanio's and Antonio's thanks.

387 **record a gift** sign over as a gift

390 **recant** take back

398 **ten more** Ten more would make up the 12 needed for a jury. In a rather sick joke, juries were sometimes called 'godfathers', because if they decided the defendant was guilty of a capital offence they were sending him 'to God'.

400 **entreat ... dinner** I beg that you will dine at my house

403 **meet** fitting

presently at once

405 **gratify** reward

411 **cope** match

The other, that he do record a gift
Here in the court, of all he dies possessed
Unto his son Lorenzo and his daughter.

DUKE He shall do this, or else I do recant
The pardon that I late pronouncèd here.

PORTIA Art thou contented Jew? What dost thou say?

SHYLOCK I am content.

PORTIA Clerk, draw a deed of gift.

SHYLOCK I pray you give me leave to go from hence.
I am not well. Send the deed after me,
And I will sign it.

DUKE Get thee gone, but do it.

GRATIANO In christening shalt thou have two godfathers;
Had I been judge, thou shouldst have had ten more,
To bring thee to the gallows, not to the font.

[*Exit* SHYLOCK

DUKE Sir I entreat you home with me to dinner.

PORTIA I humbly do desire your grace of pardon,
I must away this night toward Padua,
And it is meet I presently set forth.

DUKE I am sorry that your leisure serves you not.
Antonio, gratify this gentlemen,
For in my mind you are much bound to him.

[*Exeunt* DUKE *and his train*

BASSANIO Most worthy gentleman, I and my friend
Have by your wisdom been this day acquitted
Of grievous penalties, in lieu whereof
Three thousand ducats due unto the Jew
We freely cope your courteous pains withal.

ANTONIO And stand indebted over and above
In love and service to you evermore.

PORTIA He is well paid that is well satisfied,
And I, delivering you, am satisfied

Antonio and Bassanio press the lawyer to accept a gift. Portia asks at last for Bassanio's ring. He refuses and 'offends' her.

417 **mercenary** motivated only by the desire for money

418 **know ... meet** Portia leaves, telling Bassanio he must 'know' her (in all senses of the word) when they next meet.

420 **of force ... further** I really must try again to influence you

421 **remembrance** memento

tribute gift

423 **to pardon me** to pardon me for insisting

429 **trifle** trinket

433 **There's ... value** more hangs on this (giving up the ring) than on its monetary value

435 **proclamation** advertising

443 **'scuse** excuse

And therein do account myself well paid.
My mind was never yet more mercenary.
I pray you, know me when we meet again.
I wish you well, and so I take my leave.

BASSANIO Dear sir, of force I must attempt you further:
Take some remembrance of us as a tribute,
Not as a fee. Grant me two things I pray you,
Not to deny me, and to pardon me.

PORTIA You press me far, and therefore I will yield.
[*To* ANTONIO] Give me your gloves, I'll wear them for your sake.
[*To* BASSANIO] And for your love I'll take this ring from you.
Do not draw back your hand, I'll take no more,
And you in love shall not deny me this.

BASSANIO This ring good sir, alas, it is a trifle.
I will not shame myself to give you this.

PORTIA I will have nothing else but only this,
And now methinks I have a mind to it.

BASSANIO There's more depends on this than on the value.
The dearest ring in Venice will I give you,
And find it out by proclamation.
Only for this, I pray you, pardon me.

PORTIA I see sir, you are liberal in offers.
You taught me first to beg, and now methinks
You teach me how a beggar should be answered.

BASSANIO Good sir, this ring was given me by my wife,
And when she put it on, she made me vow
That I should neither sell, nor give, nor lose it.

PORTIA That 'scuse serves many men to save their gifts.
And if your wife be not a mad-woman,
And know how well I have deserved this ring,
She would not hold out enemy for ever
For giving it to me. Well, peace be with you.

[*Exeunt* PORTIA *and* NERISSA

Bassanio sends Gratiano after Portia to give her the ring which Portia had given him when they married. The men plan to hurry back to Belmont.

452–3 **bring ... house** persuade him, if you can, to come to Antonio's house

454 **thither presently** go to Antonio's house straight away

456 **Fly** go as fast as we can

Gratiano hands over Bassanio's ring to the 'lawyer'. Nerissa, as the 'clerk', plans to get her ring from Gratiano.

1 **Inquire ... out** Find out where the Jew lives

deed the agreement to leave money to Jessica and Lorenzo

5 **well o'erta'en** it is good that I've caught up with you

6 **upon more advice** having thought it over

ANTONIO My Lord Bassanio, let him have the ring.
Let his deservings and my love withal
Be valued 'gainst your wife's commandment.

BASSANIO Go Gratiano, run and overtake him,
Give him the ring, and bring him if thou canst
Unto Antonio's house; away, make haste.

[*Exit* GRATIANO

Come, you and I will thither presently,
And in the morning early will we both
Fly toward Belmont. Come Antonio.

[*Exeunt*

Scene 2

Venice

Enter PORTIA *and* NERISSA

PORTIA Inquire the Jew's house out, give him this deed,
And let him sign it, we'll away tonight,
And be a day before our husbands home.
This deed will be well welcome to Lorenzo.

Enter GRATIANO

GRATIANO Fair sir, you are well o'erta'en.
My Lord Bassanio upon more advice,
Hath sent you here this ring, and doth entreat
Your company at dinner.

PORTIA That cannot be.
His ring I do accept most thankfully,
And so I pray you tell him. Furthermore,
I pray you show my youth old Shylock's house.

GRATIANO That will I do.

NERISSA Sir, I would speak with you.
[*Aside to* PORTIA] I'll see if I can get my husband's ring
Which I did make him swear to keep for ever.

Portia predicts they will get the better of their husbands.

15 **old swearing** plenty of swearing (that they are speaking the truth)

17 **outface them** put them to shame

outswear them too outdo their swearing as well

PORTIA [*Aside to* NERISSA] Thou mayst, I warrant. We shall have old swearing
That they did give the rings away to men;
But we'll outface them, and outswear them too.
Away, make haste, thou know'st where I will tarry.

NERISSA Come good sir, will you show me to this house?

[*Exeunt*

Act 4 scene 1

Performance

Act 4 scene 1 is a long scene, highly dramatic and the one most people remember after seeing the play performed. Much of the drama is in the speeches of Shylock and Portia, and Shakespeare doesn't tell us very much directly about how the scene should be performed: most of the stage directions just say when people come in and go out. So we need to use our imaginations.

Work with a partner

1. Imagine that you are directing a production of this play at Shakespeare's Globe in London. (There are pictures of it on p. xiii–xvi) Think about how you would stage this scene.
2. Copy out this stage plan on a large sheet of paper:

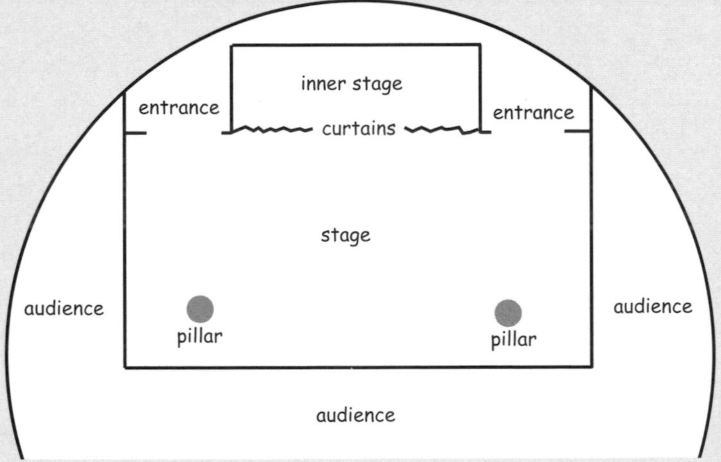

3. Mark on your plan where each of the characters would be standing or sitting at the beginning of line 17.
4. Now read through the scene and work out where the important actions take place:
   - **a** Some of these are shown by stage directions:
     Enter NERISSA dressed like a lawyer's clerk (line 118)

b Others are made clear by what people say. For example, when Bassanio says, 'Why dost thou whet (sharpen) thy knife so earnestly?' it is obvious what Shylock has started doing.

c Other actions can be worked out by the director and actors. For example, after Nerissa has handed the Duke the letter, while he reads it, Bassanio could move across to Shylock.

You can mark the main actions on a table like this:

Line	Character	Action
120	Shylock	starts to sharpen his knife
121	Duke	reads the letter
121	Bassanio	moves across to speak to Shylock

5 Take a section of between 100 and 150 lines and make a similar table of your own.

Mood temperature

There is a lot of tension in Act 4 scene 1 and the characters react emotionally to the way in which events develop. We can plot this on a mood temperature chart. For example, we can show how Bassanio's feelings develop in the scene like this:

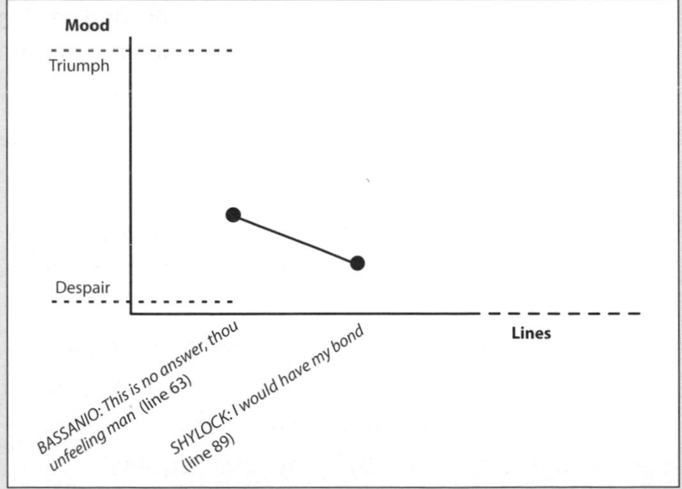

Work in a group of three or four

1 Copy out the diagram onto a long sheet of paper and fill in more points, covering lines 70–400.

2 Now make a similar chart for Shylock.

Justice and mercy

In Shakespeare's time, Shylock was the villain of *The Merchant of Venice*. Shakespeare was writing a play to rival the success of a play called *The Jew of Malta* by Marlowe. That, too, had a wicked Jew as its central character, and Shakespeare needed to compete. On the other hand, on the evidence of Act 4 scene 1 you could argue that Shylock wasn't the villain so much as the victim. There are points on both sides.

Work with a partner

1 Look again at lines 16–303. Look for evidence to support the argument that Shylock is a *villain*.

2 Set out the arguments and the evidence in a table like this:

Point	Evidence	Explanation
He admits that he hates Antonio.	...a lodged hate and a certain loathing I bear Antonio (lines 60–1)	He thinks that because he hates Antonio and has the law on his side he can hurt him as much as he likes.

3 Now look again at lines 304–99. Look for evidence to support the argument that Shylock is a *victim* and set out the arguments and evidence in a similar table.

4 Compare your two tables. On balance, do you think he comes out as:

a a villain who gets what he deserves?

b a person who is victimised by an intolerant society?

Plot summary quiz

The 12 short quotations below sum up the story of Act 4 scene 1.

1 Work out the correct order for them.

2 Work out who said each one.

A

Be merciful,
Take thrice thy money, bid me tear the bond.

B

O noble judge, O excellent young man.

C

We all expect a gentle answer Jew.

D

I pray you give me leave to go from hence,
I am not well.

E

You may as well use question with the wolf,
Why he hath made the ewe bleat for the lamb.

F

The pound of flesh which I demand of him
Is dearly bought, 'tis mine and I will have it.

G

My Lord Bassanio, let him have the ring.

H

Take some remembrance of us as a tribute,
Not as a fee.

I

And the offender's life lies in the mercy
Of the duke only, 'gainst all other voice.

J

This bond doth give thee here no jot of blood,
The words expressly are 'a pound of flesh'.

At Belmont, Lorenzo and Jessica are enjoying the moonlight and being in love. This makes them remember stories they have heard and read of lovers in myth and legend.

4 **Troilus** Lorenzo is remembering how Troilus, still in Troy longed for Cressida who was at that time with the Greeks.

7 **Thisbe** Pyramus and Thisbe were forbidden to marry. They arranged to meet, but Thisbe, who arrived first, was frightened away by a lion. When Pyramus found her scarf with blood on it he assumed the worst and killed himself. Thisbe then found his dead body and killed herself.

o'ertrip walk lightly over

10 **Dido** When Dido's husband was murdered, she escaped with his treasure. She was granted land in Africa. Later she fell in love with Aeneas who had escaped from the ruins of Troy.

13 **Medea** Medea was, for a while, Jason's wife. She made Jason's father, Aeson, young again by boiling him in a cauldron with magic herbs, gathered at night.

15–20 **Jessica ... Jew** The two lovers bring the stories of love up to date as Lorenzo and Jessica talk of their love and elopement.

16 **unthrift** spendthrift (Jessica had stolen money and jewellery from Shylock.)

Act Five

Scene 1

Belmont

Enter LORENZO *and* JESSICA

LORENZO The moon shines bright. In such a night as this,
When the sweet wind did gently kiss the trees,
And they did make no noise, in such a night
Troilus methinks mounted the Trojan walls,
And sighed his soul toward the Grecian tents
Where Cressid lay that night.

JESSICA In such a night
Did Thisbe fearfully o'ertrip the dew,
And saw the lion's shadow ere himself,
And ran dismayed away.

LORENZO In such a night
Stood Dido with a willow in her hand
Upon the wild sea banks, and waft her love
To come again to Carthage.

JESSICA In such a night
Medea gathered the enchanted herbs
That did renew old Aeson.

LORENZO In such a night
Did Jessica steal from the wealthy Jew,
And with an unthrift love did run from Venice
As far as Belmont.

JESSICA In such a night
Did young Lorenzo swear he loved her well,
Stealing her soul with many vows of faith,
And ne'er a true one.

LORENZO In such a night

Two messengers arrive separately. Stephano announces that Portia and Nerissa will arrive before dawn. He repeats Portia's pretence that she has spent the time praying. It is Launcelot who brings the news that Bassanio will be back before morning.

21 **shrew** scolding wife

23 **out-night** go on longer than you talking about nights

31–3 **By ... maid** Portia's excuse for her absence (see Act 3 scene 4 lines 27–8); the audience knows what the characters on stage do not: Portia and Nerissa have disguised themselves and rescued Antonio. This is called **dramatic irony** (see Glossary p. 239).

39 **Sola ... ho!** Launcelot is imitating first the sound of a horn to announce that he has news, and then a falconer's cry to a hawk.

43 **Leave holloaing man** Stop making this noise (As usual Launcelot has gone on rather too long for his hearers.)

46 **post** messenger

47 **horn ... news** the cornucopia, or horn of plenty

Did pretty Jessica, like a little shrew,
Slander her love, and he forgave it her.

JESSICA I would out-night you, did no body come.
But hark, I hear the footing of a man.

Enter STEPHANO

LORENZO Who comes so fast in silence of the night?

STEPHANO A friend.

LORENZO A friend? What friend? Your name I pray you, friend?

STEPHANO Stephano is my name, and I bring word
My mistress will before the break of day
Be here at Belmont; she doth stray about
By holy crosses where she kneels and prays
For happy wedlock hours.

LORENZO Who comes with her?

STEPHANO None but a holy hermit and her maid.
I pray you is my master yet returned?

LORENZO He is not, nor we have not heard from him.
But go we in I pray thee Jessica,
And ceremoniously let us prepare
Some welcome for the mistress of the house.

Enter LAUNCELOT

LAUNCELOT Sola, sola! Woo ha ho! Sola, sola!

LORENZO Who calls?

LAUNCELOT Sola! Did you see Master Lorenzo?
Master Lorenzo, sola, sola!

LORENZO Leave halloaing man, here.

LAUNCELOT Sola! Where, where?

LORENZO Here.

LAUNCELOT Tell him there's a post come from my master, with his horn full of good news: my master will be here ere morning.

[*Exit*

Lorenzo and Jessica stay outside. He sends Stephano in to instruct the musicians to play while they wait for Portia's arrival. Lorenzo talks about the power of music.

49 **expect** wait for

51 **signify** tell people

57 **Become** are suitable for

touches playing, fingering the strings

58 **floor of heaven** the night sky

59 **patens** plates of silver or gold used at the communion service (Some editions read 'patterns' which makes equally good sense.)

60 **orb** star or planet

61 **But** which does not

motion The sun, moon and planets were thought to be in hollow globes, which, as they revolved, made harmonious sounds – 'the music of the spheres'.

62 **quiring** making music

cherubins cherubs, angels

63 **Such ... souls** the same harmony exists in the souls of men

64–5 **muddy ... it in** while the body still keeps the soul of every man imprisoned

65 **it** the harmony

66 **wake Diana** keep watch for your mistress (Diana was goddess of the moon and of chastity.)

70 **spirits are attentive** emotions are more aware

71 **wanton** frisky

72 **race ... colts** herd of young horses which have not yet been broken in

77 **make ... stand** they will stand still all at the same time

LORENZO Sweet soul, let's in, and there expect their coming.
And yet no matter – why should we go in?
My friend Stephano, signify I pray you
Within the house, your mistress is at hand,
And bring your music forth into the air.

[*Exit* STEPHANO

How sweet the moonlight sleeps upon this bank.
Here will we sit, and let the sounds of music
Creep in our ears. Soft stillness and the night
Become the touches of sweet harmony.
Sit Jessica. Look how the floor of heaven
Is thick inlaid with patens of bright gold.
There's not the smallest orb which thou behold'st
But in his motion like an angel sings,
Still quiring to the young-eyed cherubins;
Such harmony is in immortal souls,
But whilst this muddy vesture of decay
Doth grossly close it in, we cannot hear it.

Enter Musicians

Come ho, and wake Diana with a hymn,
With sweetest touches pierce your mistress' ear,
And draw her home with music.

[*Music*

JESSICA I am never merry when I hear sweet music.

LORENZO The reason is your spirits are attentive.
For do but note a wild and wanton herd,
Or race of youthful and unhandled colts,
Fetching mad bounds, bellowing and neighing
loud,
Which is the hot condition of their blood;
If they but hear perchance a trumpet sound,
Or any air of music touch their ears,
You shall perceive them make a mutual stand,
Their savage eyes turned to a modest gaze
By the sweet power of music. Therefore the poet

Lorenzo claims that a man with no musical sense is likely to be dull and treacherous. Portia and Nerissa, wearing their own clothes, approach the house, obviously content to be back.

80 **Did feign** claimed

Orpheus In Greek myth, Orpheus was able to charm with his music even inanimate objects and forces of nature.

81 **nought so stockish** nothing is so unfeeling

83–5 **The man ... spoils** A man unable to be moved by music is capable of betrayal and has violent and destructive tendencies

84 **concord** harmony

86 **The ... night** his emotions are dull and dark

87 **Erebus** In Greek myth one of the oldest of the gods: Darkness.

88 **Mark** Pay attention to

91 **naughty** evil, wicked (not the weaker meaning it has today)

93 **So ... less** A stronger light makes the weaker light seem dull

95–7 **state ... waters** the apparent importance of a man soon disappears in the face of someone really significant; in the same way a small stream is completely lost when it runs into the sea

99 **Nothing ... respect** I understand that nothing is good without reference to the circumstance

103 **attended** paid attention

107 **How ... are** The effect depends on circumstances

109 **Peace ho** Portia's greeting also tells the musicians to stop playing.

Endymion In Greek myth, this was a beautiful young man loved by the moon goddess who made sure he would sleep forever, so that she could always visit him.

Did feign that Orpheus drew trees, stones, and
  floods;
Since naught so stockish, hard, and full of rage,
But music for the time doth change his nature.
The man that hath no music in himself,
Nor is not moved with concord of sweet sounds,
Is fit for treasons, stratagems, and spoils;
The motions of his spirit are dull as night,
And his affections dark as Erebus:
Let no such man be trusted. Mark the music.

Enter PORTIA *and* NERISSA

PORTIA That light we see is burning in my hall.
How far that little candle throws his beams,
So shines a good deed in a naughty world.

NERISSA When the moon shone we did not see the candle.

PORTIA So doth the greater glory dim the less.
A substitute shines brightly as a king
Until a king be by, and then his state
Empties itself, as doth an inland brook
Into the main of waters. Music, hark.

NERISSA It is your music, madam, of the house.

PORTIA Nothing is good I see without respect,
Methinks it sounds much sweeter than by day.

NERISSA Silence bestows that virtue on it, madam.

PORTIA The crow doth sing as sweetly as the lark
When neither is attended; and I think
The nightingale, if she should sing by day
When every goose is cackling, would be thought
No better a musician than the wren.
How many things by season seasoned are
To their right praise and true perfection.
Peace ho, the moon sleeps with Endymion,
And would not be awaked.

[*Music ceases*

Portia and Nerissa are welcomed home. They are pleased to learn that their husbands are not back yet and Portia instructs her servants and Lorenzo and Jessica not to mention that they have been away. Shortly afterwards they welcome their returning husbands and Antonio.

115 **speed** prosper

119–20 **Give ... hence** tell my servants not to indicate that we have been absent

SD *tucket* personal trumpet call, the signal for Bassanio's arrival

127–8 **We ... sun** If you were always to walk in the night it would be daytime here for us just as it is on the other side of the world

129–30 **light** Portia plays on the word 'light'. A light (frivolous) wife might not be faithful to her husband.

132 **But God sort all** Let God decide

135–7 **bound** Bassanio and Portia play on the word 'bound'. Bassanio uses it to mean 'indebted' and 'close in friendship'. Portia repeats the meaning of 'indebted, obliged' and in the third use of the word suggests that Antonio had 'pledged' his life to Shylock and was also held 'bound' in prison. (see Glossary for **play on words**, and **pun** p. 242)

LORENZO That is the voice,
Or I am much deceived, of Portia.

PORTIA He knows me as the blind man knows the cuckoo –
By the bad voice.

LORENZO Dear lady welcome home.

PORTIA We have been praying for our husbands' welfare,
Which speed, we hope, the better for our words.
Are they returned?

LORENZO Madam, they are not yet;
But there is come a messenger before
To signify their coming.

PORTIA Go in Nerissa;
Give order to my servants that they take
No note at all of our being absent hence –
Nor you, Lorenzo – Jessica, nor you.

[A tucket sounds

LORENZO Your husband is at hand, I hear his trumpet.
We are no tell-tales madam, fear you not.

PORTIA This night methinks is but the daylight sick,
It looks a little paler; 'tis a day,
Such as the day is when the sun is hid.

Enter BASSANIO, ANTONIO, GRATIANO, *and their followers*

BASSANIO We should hold day with the Antipodes,
If you would walk in absence of the sun.

PORTIA Let me give light, but let me not be light;
For a light wife doth make a heavy husband,
And never be Bassanio so for me.
But God sort all. You are welcome home my lord.

BASSANIO I thank you madam. Give welcome to my friend.
This is the man, this is Antonio,
To whom I am so infinitely bound.

PORTIA You should in all sense be much bound to him,
For as I hear he was much bound for you.

A quarrel starts between Gratiano and Nerissa over her ring. Portia joins in, saying she is sure Bassanio still has hers.

138 **acquitted of** repaid

140 **It** The welcome

141 **Therefore ... courtesy** so I will stop merely speaking words of welcome

144 **gelt** castrated

147 **paltry** insignificant, worthless

148 **posy** inscription round the inside of a ring

149 **cutler's poetry** doggerel (badly written) verse, such as might be inscribed on a knife handle

150 **leave** abandon, part with (the ring)

155–6 **Though ... respective** Even if you didn't care about me you should have remembered the intense promises you made

156 **respective** careful of it

158 **The clerk ... it** The clerk you gave it to will never have a beard (he gave it to a woman)

on's on his

159 **an if** if

162 **scrubbed** stunted

164 **prating** chattering, talkative

167 **slightly** carelessly

ANTONIO No more than I am well acquitted of.

PORTIA Sir, you are very welcome to our house.
It must appear in other ways than words,
Therefore I scant this breathing courtesy.

GRATIANO [*To* NERISSA] By yonder moon I swear you do me wrong,
In faith I gave it to the judge's clerk.
Would he were gelt that had it for my part,
Since you do take it, love, so much at heart.

PORTIA A quarrel ho, already? What's the matter?

GRATIANO About a hoop of gold, a paltry ring
That she did give me, whose posy was
For all the world like cutler's poetry
Upon a knife, 'Love me, and leave me not.'

NERISSA What talk you of the posy or the value?
You swore to me when I did give it you,
That you would wear it till your hour of death,
And that it should lie with you in your grave.
Though not for me, yet for your vehement oaths,
You should have been respective and have kept it.
Gave it a judge's clerk? No, God's my judge,
The clerk will ne'er wear hair on's face that had it.

GRATIANO He will, and if he live to be a man.

NERISSA Ay, if a woman live to be a man.

GRATIANO Now by this hand I gave it to a youth,
A kind of boy, a little scrubbed boy,
No higher than thyself, the judge's clerk,
A prating boy that begged it as a fee.
I could not for my heart deny it him.

PORTIA You were to blame, I must be plain with you,
To part so slightly with your wife's first gift,
A thing stuck on with oaths upon your finger,
And so riveted with faith unto your flesh.
I gave my love a ring, and made him swear
Never to part with it, and here he stands.

Bassanio realises he is in a fix and Gratiano now unkindly gives him away. Portia threatens not to sleep with Bassanio until she sees the ring. Bassanio tries to explain.

173–4 **for ... masters** for all the money in the world

176 **An't ... it** If it happened to me I'd be frantic

185 **Not ... hope** I hope not the one

189 **void** empty

195 **would conceive** could imagine

196 **left** parted with

198 **abate ... displeasure** not be so deeply offended by what I have done

199 **virtue** power

201 **contain** keep

I dare be sworn for him he would not leave it,
Nor pluck it from his finger, for the wealth
That the world masters. Now in faith Gratiano,
You give your wife too unkind a cause of grief.
An't were to me, I should be mad at it.

BASSANIO [*Aside*] Why, I were best to cut my left hand off,
And swear I lost the ring defending it.

GRATIANO My Lord Bassanio gave his ring away
Unto the judge that begged it, and indeed
Deserved it too. And then the boy his clerk
That took some pains in writing, he begged mine,
And neither man nor master would take aught
But the two rings.

PORTIA What ring gave you, my lord?
Not that, I hope, which you received of me.

BASSANIO If I could add a lie unto a fault,
I would deny it; but you see my finger
Hath not the ring upon it, it is gone.

PORTIA Even so void is your false heart of truth.
By heaven I will ne'er come in your bed
Until I see the ring.

NERISSA Nor I in yours
Till I again see mine.

BASSANIO Sweet Portia,
If you did know to whom I gave the ring,
If you did know for whom I gave the ring,
And would conceive for what I gave the ring
And how unwillingly I left the ring,
When nought would be accepted but the ring,
You would abate the strength of your displeasure.

PORTIA If you had known the virtue of the ring,
Or half her worthiness that gave the ring,
Or your own honour to contain the ring,
You would not then have parted with the ring.
What man is there so much unreasonable,

Bassanio explains what happened. Portia and Nerissa swear that if these 'men' turn up they'll sleep with them. Antonio, who persuaded Bassanio to part with the ring, is embarrassed.

205 **terms of zeal** enthusiasm, conviction

wanted the modesty that would have lacked the restraint to go on demanding something kept as a symbol

210 **civil doctor** doctor of civil law

213 **suffered** allowed

214 **held up** saved

217 **beset … courtesy** covered in shame and with a need to do the courteous thing

220 **candles ... night** stars

226 **liberal** generous

230 **Argus** a monster with a hundred eyes

237 **mar ... pen** both damage his pen (he is a clerk) and castrate him

If you had pleased to have defended it
With any terms of zeal, wanted the modesty
To urge the thing held as a ceremony?
Nerissa teaches me what to believe:
I'll die for't, but some woman had the ring.

BASSANIO No by my honour madam, by my soul
No woman had it, but a civil doctor,
Which did refuse three thousand ducats of me,
And begged the ring, the which I did deny him,
And suffered him to go displeased away,
Even he that had held up the very life
Of my dear friend. What should I say sweet lady?
I was enforced to send it after him;
I was beset with shame and courtesy;
My honour would not let ingratitude
So much besmear it. Pardon me good lady,
For by these blessed candles of the night,
Had you been there, I think you would have
  begged
The ring of me to give the worthy doctor.

PORTIA Let not that doctor e'er come near my house.
Since he hath got the jewel that I loved,
And that which you did swear to keep for me,
I will become as liberal as you;
I'll not deny him anything I have,
No, not my body, nor my husband's bed.
Know him I shall, I am well sure of it.
Lie not a night from home. Watch me like Argus.
If you do not, if I be left alone,
Now by mine honour, which is yet mine own,
I'll have that doctor for my bedfellow.

NERISSA And I his clerk. Therefore be well advised
How you do leave me to mine own protection.

GRATIANO Well, do you so. Let not me take him then,
For if I do, I'll mar the young clerk's pen.

Bassanio swears he will never again break faith with Portia. Antonio guarantees his word and Portia gives him the same ring again. They explain.

240 **enforced** that I could not help

244–5 **In both ... self** Bassanio sees himself reflected in both of Portia's eyes. She teases him by suggesting that this makes him two-faced, so that 'And there's an oath of credit' is heavily ironic (for **irony**, see Glossary p. 241).

246 **of credit** to be believed

251 **Had quite miscarried** would have been completely lost

252 **My ... forfeit** my soul as the penalty

253 **advisedly** consciously

254 **surety** guarantor Antonio will guarantee that Bassanio will keep his promise.

262 **In lieu of** in return for

263–5 **Why ... deserved it?** Portia and Nerissa each claim to have slept with the 'man' to whom her ring was given. Gratiano jokingly states that the women have thus cheated on them before they could possibly have deserved such treatment. In just the same way, he says, as the roads are mended in summer before winter has put them into a bad state of repair.

265 **cuckolds** husbands who have been betrayed by their wives

266 **grossly** coarsely

amazed bewildered

ANTONIO I am the unhappy subject of these quarrels.

PORTIA Sir, grieve not you, you are welcome
notwithstanding.

BASSANIO Portia, forgive me this enforced wrong,
And, in the hearing of these many friends
I swear to thee, even by thine own fair eyes
Wherein I see myself –

PORTIA Mark you but that?
In both my eyes he doubly sees himself,
In each eye, one – swear by your double self,
And there's an oath of credit.

BASSANIO Nay, but hear me.
Pardon this fault, and by my soul I swear
I never more will break an oath with thee.

ANTONIO I once did lend my body for his wealth,
Which but for him that had your husband's ring
Had quite miscarried. I dare be bound again,
My soul upon the forfeit, that your lord
Will never more break faith advisedly.

PORTIA Then you shall be his surety. Give him this,
And bid him keep it better than the other.

ANTONIO Here Lord Bassanio, swear to keep this ring.

BASSANIO By heaven it is the same I gave the doctor.

PORTIA I had it of him. Pardon me, Bassanio,
For by this ring the doctor lay with me.

NERISSA And pardon me my gentle Gratiano,
For that same scrubbed boy the doctor's clerk,
In lieu of this last night did lie with me.

GRATIANO Why this is like the mending of highways
In summer where the ways are fair enough.
What, are we cuckolds ere we have deserved it?

PORTIA Speak not so grossly. You are all amazed.
Here is a letter, read it at your leisure –

There is a letter for Antonio about his ships, three of which have suddenly reached harbour. There is also the special deed of gift for Lorenzo and Jessica.

272 **even but now** only just a moment ago

286 **life and living** 'Life' because of the business in court, and 'living' because of the news that he is still in business.

288 **road** safe anchorage

294 **manna** the food that God sent from heaven to feed the Israelites in the desert

296–7 **you ... full** you haven't yet heard enough detail about these events

298 **charge ... inter'gatories** you can take statements from us

It comes from Padua from Bellario –
There you shall find that Portia was the doctor,
Nerissa there her clerk. Lorenzo here
Shall witness I set forth as soon as you,
And even but now returned. I have not yet
Entered my house. Antonio you are welcome,
And I have better news in store for you
Than you expect. Unseal this letter soon,
There you shall find three of your argosies
Are richly come to harbour suddenly.
You shall not know by what strange accident
I chanced on this letter.

ANTONIO I am dumb.

BASSANIO Were you the doctor, and I knew you not?

GRATIANO Were you the clerk that is to make me cuckold?

NERISSA Ay but the clerk that never means to do it,
Unless he live until he be a man.

BASSANIO Sweet doctor, you shall be my bedfellow:
When I am absent, then lie with my wife.

ANTONIO Sweet lady, you have given me life and living;
For here I read for certain that my ships
Are safely come to road.

PORTIA How now, Lorenzo?
My clerk hath some good comforts too for you.

NERISSA Ay, and I'll give them him without a fee.
There do I give to you and Jessica
From the rich Jew, a special deed of gift
After his death, of all he dies possessed of.

LORENZO Fair ladies, you drop manna in the way
Of starved people.

PORTIA It is almost morning,
And yet I am sure you are not satisfied
Of these events at full. Let us go in,
And charge us there upon inter'gatories,
And we will answer all things faithfully.

Gratiano offers Nerissa the choice of going to bed for the remaining two hours of the night, or waiting until the next night. He will always be sure to keep her ring safely.

302 **stay** wait

304 **were ... come** if it were already day

305 **That I were** so that I could be

306–7 **I'll ... as** nothing will concern me more than

GRATIANO Let it be so. The first inter'gatory
That my Nerissa shall be sworn on is
Whether till the next night she had rather stay,
Or go to bed now, being two hours to day.
But were the day come, I should wish it dark
That I were couching with the doctor's clerk.
Well, while I live I'll fear no other thing
So sore, as keeping safe Nerissa's ring.

[*Exeunt*

Act 5 scene 1

A man's world?

You could argue that *The Merchant of Venice* is a play about men and the things that they are interested in: money, law, and power. The central plot is about a conflict between two men, Shylock and Antonio.

Work with a partner

1 Use a point/evidence/explanation table. In the first column list the reasons why in this play it's 'a man's world'.

2 In the second column, write a short quotation or an action in the play that backs it up.

3 In the right hand column explain why the quotation or action supports the argument, for example:

Point	Evidence	Explanation
The central conflict is about two men, Antonio and Shylock.	SHYLOCK: If I can catch him once upon the hip I will feed fat the ancient grudge I bear him (Act 1 scene 1 lines 43–4)	This speech of Shylock's is all about the world of business*men*.

On the other hand, as we see in Acts 4 and 5, the men don't have it all their own way. Where would Antonio and his friends have been without Portia? (But then again, she had to dress up as a man to help them out.)

4 Make a second point/evidence/explanation table to list the ways in which the women prove their importance.

Bringing the two sides together

Work in a group of four

1 Share your tables and ideas.

2 Prepare a presentation for the rest of the class in answer to this question:
How fair is *The Merchant of Venice* in the way it treats women?

Quotation quiz

For each of these quotations, work out:

1 who said it
2 who they were speaking to
3 what it tells us about:
   a the speaker
   b the situation
   c any other characters.

A You should in all sense be much bound to him, For as I hear he was much bound for you.

B How sweet the moonlight sleeps upon this bank.

C Fair ladies, you drop manna in the way Of starved people.

D A quarrel ho, already? What's the matter?

E Lie not a night from home. Watch me like Argus.

F How far that little candle throws his beams, So shines a good deed in a naughty world.

G For here I read for certain that my ships Are safely come to road.

H By heaven it is the same I gave the doctor.

I There you shall find that Portia was the doctor, Nerissa there her clerk.

J Pardon this fault, and by my soul I swear I never more will break an oath with thee.

Act 1
Antonio, a merchant, agrees to borrow money from Shylock, a Jewish money-lender, to help his friend Bassanio. Bassanio wishes to marry Portia, a rich and beautiful young woman. Shylock complains about Antonio's previous treatment of him, but says he will offer the loan on these terms: if Antonio does not pay, he must forfeit a pound of his flesh. Antonio agrees. At Belmont, Portia complains of her situation. Her deceased father left instructions that she may only marry someone who successfully chooses the correct casket from a choice of three. The correct one contains Portia's portrait.
Act 2
The Prince of Morocco arrives to attempt the casket challenge. Launcelot Gobbo, Shylock's servant, meets his father and together they convince Bassanio to employ Launcelot. Jessica, Shylock's daughter, sends a letter to Lorenzo, with whom she plans to elope. While Shylock is at dinner she escapes, dressed as a boy, and leaves Venice. We hear that Shylock is greatly disturbed by Jessica's leaving. The Prince of Morocco fails the casket test, as does the Prince of Arragon. Bassanio sets sail for Belmont.
Act 3
Shylock speaks of how being a Jew makes him no less human than if he were a Christian. He learns that Jessica has been wasteful with the money she took from him, and that one of Antonio's ships is wrecked. He decides to pursue Antonio for the pound of flesh if he is unable to pay his debt. Bassanio arrives at Belmont and chooses the right casket. Portia gives Bassanio a ring as a token of her love. Gratiano and Nerissa also decide to get married. Bassanio learns that Antonio is in danger because he cannot repay the debt, and leaves for Venice. Portia hatches a plan to help Antonio.
Act 4
At Antonio's trial Portia arrives disguised as Balthasar, a male lawyer. She agrees that the contract cannot be broken, but asks Shylock to show mercy. He refuses. She tells him he must remove exactly a pound of flesh, and cannot spill any blood. If he does not stick to this he will be executed. Shylock unsuccessfully tries to back down and take the money he is owed. He is forced to give up his wealth, half to the state and half to Antonio. He is also forced to convert to Christianity. Antonio allows him to keep half his wealth. Portia and Nerissa demand of Bassanio and Gratiano the rings they gave them earlier, as payment for their legal services. Eventually, they give them the rings.
Act 5
Back at Belmont, Jessica and Lorenzo talk about famous lovers from literature. Portia and Nerissa return from Venice, as do Bassanio and Gratiano. Portia and Nerissa feign anger that their husbands have given away their rings. They eventually explain their trick. We learn that Antonio's ships have safely arrived.

Act/ Scene	Action	Theme/Summary
1.1	Antonio agrees to lend Bassanio money.	Finance; Antonio's devotion to Bassanio.
1.2	Portia complains that she must marry whoever wins the casket challenge.	Bonds; the constraints on Portia.
1.3	Despite the way he has been treated, Shylock agrees to lend money to Antonio.	Usury; stereotypes and prejudice.
2.1	The Prince of Morocco arrives.	Bonds and obligations.
2.2	Launcelot Gobbo fools his father. Bassanio agrees to employ Launcelot.	Launcelot's comic speech and clowning.
2.3	Jessica gives Launcelot a letter to deliver.	Jessica's plan to elope; Shylock's home life.
2.4	Lorenzo and friends prepare for a masque. Lorenzo explains the plan to elope.	Appearances and deception.
2.5	Shylock tells Jessica to lock up the house while he goes out for dinner.	Shylock's disapproval of extravagance.
2.6	Jessica runs away from home dressed as a boy.	Appearances and deception; theft of Shylock's money.
2.7	Morocco fails the casket test.	Appearances and deception
2.8	Solanio and Salerio report Shylock's reaction to Jessica's flight.	Shylock's feelings of despair.
2.9	The Prince of Arragon fails the casket test. Portia hears of Bassanio's arrival.	Arragon's self-importance; appearances and deception.
3.1	Shylock describes his common humanity, and hears of Jessica's extravagance.	Stereotypes and prejudice; Shylock's feelings of anger.
3.2	Bassanio chooses the right casket.	Appearances and deception.
3.3	Shylock has Antonio arrested.	Shylock's revenge.
3.4	Portia's plan to help Antonio.	Appearances and deception.
3.5	Launcelot, Jessica and Lorenzo talk.	Launcelot's prejudice.
4.1	Antonio appears before the Duke and is rescued by Portia. Shylock is crushed.	Portia's trickery.
4.2	Gratiano gives Bassanio's ring to Portia.	Portia's trickery continues.
5.1	The lovers return to Belmont. Gratiano and Bassanio learn the truth about the rings.	Appearances and deception; forgiveness.

In this section of the book there are activities and advice to help you explore the play in more detail:

On pages 238–44 there is a Glossary, which explains some of the technical terms that are used in the book.

Character

The Merchant of Venice is a play with some of the most famous characters in literature. There are characters from many levels of society. There are rich characters like Antonio, Tubal and Portia. In contrast, there are poorer characters like Gobbo and his father. There are a few female characters among a majority of male characters, and there are also Christian and Jewish characters. The characters are revealed by what they say and do.

Who said what?

The main way in which Shakespeare communicates the thoughts and feelings of his character is through the words he gives them to say. These often give us clues about the kind of person they are.

Work on your own

1 Match the quotation to the character. Try to do each one without looking it up in the text of the play.

Characters:

Shylock Portia Antonio Bassanio Jessica

Quotations:

- **a** *I had it of Leah when I was a bachelor. I would not have given it for a wilderness of monkeys.* (Act 3 scene 1 lines 115–17)
- **b** *For I am much ashamed of my exchange. | But love is blind...* (Act 2 scene 6 lines 35–6)

c *Come on, in this there can be no dismay, | My ships come home a month before the day.* (Act 1 scene 3 lines 177–8)

d *By my troth Nerissa, my little body is aweary of this great world.* (Act 1 scene 2 lines 1–2)

e *Tis not unknown to you Antonio, | How much I have disabled mine estate...* (Act 1 scene 1 lines 122–3)

What does it tell us?

When you find a useful character quotation there are several questions you can use to help you explore the information it contains. Look at the example below:

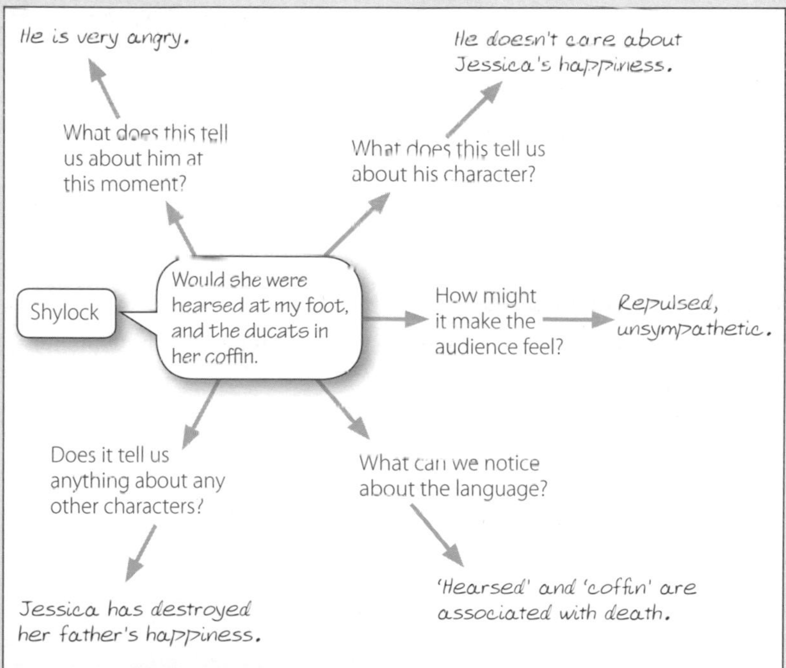

Work with a partner

1. Choose one of the quotations from the five listed in the previous question. Discuss what it tells you about that character.
2. Take a large sheet of paper and make a similar diagram to the one above.

Development

Work with a partner

1 Here are some more quotations. Again, match the quotation to the character.

a *Tarry Jew, | The law hath yet another hold on you.* (Act 4 scene 1 lines 345–6)

b *The Jew shall have my flesh, blood, bones, and all, | Ere thou shalt lose for me one drop of blood.* (Act 4 scene 1 lines 112–13)

c *...for this favour, | He presently become a Christian* (Act 4 scene 1 lines 385–6)

d *I am sorry thou wilt leave my father so: | Our house is hell, and thou, a merry devil, | Didst rob it of some taste of tediousness.* (Act 2 scene 3 lines 1–3)

e *I am as like to call thee so again, | To spit on thee again, to spurn thee too.* (Act 1 scene 3 lines 127–8)

2 Choose one of these quotations and make a diagram like the one on the previous page.

Building a character

When you are studying a character in a play you can begin by making a list of key quotations. These:

- should tell you something important about the character
- should each tell you something different about the character
- can be spoken by the character or about the character
- should be as short as possible.

Work on your own

1 Make a list of key quotations for the character of Shylock. Write down:

a the words of the quotation

b the act/scene/line numbers.

Work in a group of three or four

2 Share your quotations. Decide on the top six quotations about Shylock.

3 For each quotation work out:
   a what it tells us about Shylock
   b what it tells us about any other characters
   c anything important about the language used.
4 Share your ideas with the rest of the class.

Character web page

Many of the characters in the play are important people, or well-known people, in the world of the play. Many famous and important people in the twenty-first century have their own websites. The web page might include information about the person, a section on likes and dislikes, a section with links to other websites, and include a status update. This is how a web page for Antonio might look:

Work with a partner

1 Pick a character from the play and design a similar web page. You can do this on paper or a computer. Try to make it as appropriate as possible based on what you know from the play.
2 Present it to the class.

Character types

The Merchant of Venice is a comedy. Even though Shakespeare has created characters with unique attributes, traditional character types can be seen. A controlling old rich father who is tricked by their child is a character type that can be found in plays from as long ago as Ancient Greece. Elements of this can be seen in the story of Shylock and Jessica.

Here are some other character types:

The fairytale princess
A young, rich and beautiful woman who falls in love and marries.

The cold-hearted villain
A character who is excessively wicked and inventive in his/her evil.

The captive princess
A young woman who is trapped by the villain and must be rescued.

The trickster
A character who is often a loner. S/he knows the rules of society but tries to ignore them, or manipulate them for his/her own benefit.

The adventurer
A character who risks everything in pursuit of wealth or treasure.

Work in a small group

1. For each of the character types listed above, think of at least one character from a TV or film story who fits this description.
2. Can you think of any other character types who regularly turn up in TV or film stories?
3. Which of all these character types can be found in *The Merchant of Venice*?
4. Copy and complete this table:

Character type	Character in *The Merchant of Venice*	Your evidence
The fairytale princess		
The cold-hearted villain		
The captive princess		

The trickster		
The adventurer		

Development

Work in a group of three or four

1 Discuss these questions:

- **a** Why might Shakespeare have chosen to use character types which his audience would recognise?
- **b** Why might these character types still be used in entertainment today?
- **c** Of course, Shakespeare doesn't just take the character types as they are. He changes them to fit into his story, and he makes them more complicated and interesting. Pick one of the characters in the middle column of your table. Explain how s/he is more complex and interesting than a character type.

2 Present your ideas to the class.

The whole story

Work in a group of three or four

1 Create a poster or leaflet that conveys information and analysis of a character in *The Merchant of Venice*. It could include:

- **a** quotations said *by* the character
- **b** quotations said *about* the character
- **c** what these quotations suggest to the audience/reader about the character
- **d** interesting aspects of the character's language
- **e** how the audience feels about the character at different times in the play
- **f** other characters from modern texts/films/programmes who share similar characteristics.

2 Present your poster to the rest of the class.

Drama and performance

Shakespeare intended his plays to be performed. Every theatre production is unique. How a play is performed can highlight some aspects of the play over others. For example, early productions tended to portray Shylock as a comedy villain. More recent productions have portrayed Shylock as a more sympathetic character. This section begins with some drama games to help you explore a variety of performance options.

Styles of performance

This is a fun game that highlights how a change in the way a line is said can alter the tone of a dialogue.

Work with a partner

1 Pick one of these groups:
- Hairdressers
- Gangsters
- Clowns
- Teenagers
- Hooligans

2 Practise saying these lines in the style of your chosen group.

a Act 1 scene 1 lines 1–14

b Act 1 scene 2 lines 80–96

c Act 3 scene 1 lines 101–23

3 Perform to the class. They should try to guess which style you chose.

On the psychiatrist's couch

Work in a group of three or four

1 Two members of the group are psychiatrists. The other person is a character from the play who has decided they need therapy at a particular moment in the play. Choose from these situations:

a Antonio just before the trial

b Portia before Bassanio arrives

c Shylock deciding whether to lend Antonio money.

2 The 'psychiatrists' should try to work out the emotional and mental state of the character by asking questions about:
- what has happened previously
- what might happen next
- what the character wants
- what the character fears.

Freeze-frames

A freeze-frame is like a living photograph of a moment in the play. It can communicate the relationships between characters. It can also show how characters might feel at that moment, and give an indication of what they might do next.

Work in a group of three or four

1 Create a freeze-frame for one of these scenarios:
  a Shylock agrees to convert to Christianity
  b Bassanio is deciding which casket to choose
  c Jessica escapes from Shylock's house.

2 Present your freeze-frame to the class.

Move to punctuation

This game is a good way of exploring pace and rhythm in Shakespeare's language.

Work in a group of four

1 Choose one of these sections:
  a Act 1 scene 3 lines 100–38
  b Act 3 scene 2 lines 243–302
  c Act 4 scene 1 lines 207–88

2 Cast the parts.

3 Read the scene aloud taking note of the following:
  a The person who is reading must walk and talk.
  b Every time there is a punctuation mark, s/he must change direction.
  c Everyone else stays still until it is their turn to speak.

Motivations

A powerful technique for performance is to decide on a character's motivation in a scene, and to perform accordingly. However, the character's motivations must be supported by the text.

Work with a partner

1 Look at Act 5 scene 1 lines 1–24. This extract could be performed in a number of different ways:

	Jessica	Lorenzo
1	She wants to get Lorenzo to kiss her.	He's decided he no longer loves her and wishes she wasn't with him.
2	She loves Lorenzo deeply.	He loves Jessica deeply.
3	She is unsure whether she has done the right thing.	He's beginning to think that Jessica has changed her mind.

2 Cast the parts. Each choose one of the three motivations in the list.

3 Act the scene out interpreting the lines to fit the motivation you have chosen. Think about: tone of voice, movement, gesture, and facial expression.

4 Now each choose a different motivation and try the scene again.

5 Talk about how the two versions went. Did one fit the lines better? If so, why?

Extension activity

Work with a partner

1 Choose a scene from this list:

- **a** Act 1 scene 1 lines 140–85
- **b** Act 1 scene 3 lines 50–99
- **c** Act 2 scene 2 lines 32–80
- **d** Act 3 scene 1 lines 93–124
- **e** Act 5 scene 1 lines 192–233

2 Read and discuss the scene. What different motivations could each of the two characters have in it?

3 Copy and complete this table, setting out your ideas:

Scene:		
	Character 1	**Character 2**
1		
2		
3		

4 Cast the parts. Each choose one of the three motivations in the list.

5 Act the scene out interpreting the lines to fit the motivation you have chosen.

6 Now each choose a different motivation and try the scene again.

7 Talk about how the two versions went. Did one fit the lines better? If so, why?

Writing follow-up

Work on your own

1 Choose one of the scenes you have worked on. Use a diagram like this to make notes about the motivations you used in that scene:

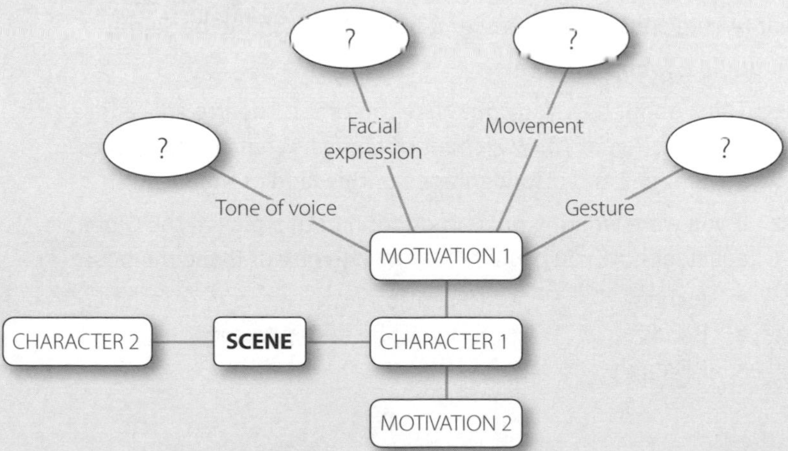

2 Now imagine that you are the director of a production of the play. One of your actors is unwell and cannot attend rehearsals. Use your notes as the basis for an email to him or her, explaining how you would like this scene to be performed.

Performance space

Look at the illustration on p. xiv. It is of the reconstructed Globe Theatre, which is the type of theatre in use when Shakespeare was writing. It is a round, roofless theatre and it has a stage which projects out into the audience. This style of stage is called a **thrust stage** (see Glossary p. 244).

Shakespeare's plays are still performed at this theatre. They are usually performed in daylight, and the audience and the actors can see each other clearly. Sets are usually very simple.

Work with a partner

1 Discuss why a production of *The Merchant of Venice* on this stage might differ from a film production or a production in a more modern theatre.

2 Share your ideas with the class.

Set and costume design at Shakespeare's Globe

The design of a set can be used to communicate a theme. For example, a set trying to highlight the theme of money might have a large gold coin at its centre, or a bank facade in the background.

Work in a group of three

1 Think about how you could use the Globe Theatre space for a production of *The Merchant of Venice*. What would be the advantages and disadvantages of this kind of theatre?

2 If you were working on a production of this play at the Globe, consider how you could communicate **one** of these themes:

- Justice
- Bonds
- Revenge
- Deception
- Christianity and Judaism

3 Talk about what settings, costumes and properties you might use.

4 Present your ideas to the rest of the class.

Set and costume design in a modern indoor theatre

Work in a group of three

1 Think about how you could use a modern indoor theatre space for a production of *The Merchant of Venice*. Compared to the Globe Theatre, what would be the advantages and disadvantages?

2 Choose another theme from the list opposite and discuss how you could communicate it in this kind of theatre.

3 Talk about what settings, costumes, and properties you might use.

4 Present your ideas to the rest of the class.

Writing task

Work on your own

1 Imagine you are directing a production of *The Merchant of Venice*.

2 Choose a scene from the play.

3 Decide whether you want to create a production for the theatre, for TV, or for film. If you choose theatre, decide what kind of theatre.

4 Write a letter to the production designer, explaining what you want in terms of:

- scenery
- costumes
- lighting
- music
- recorded sounds.

5 Write a paragraph for each actor, explaining what you think the motivation for the character is and explain why. Include detailed notes on how you think some (up to five) of their lines should be performed. Refer to:

- tone of voice
- movement
- facial expression
- gestures.

Themes and issues

'I will have my bond'

The word 'bond' is used more than 30 times in this play. It has different meanings at different times.

Work on your own

1 Look up the word 'bond' in a dictionary.

2 Write down the different meanings it gives.

3 Which of these applies to 'bonds' in *The Merchant of Venice*?

Characters' bonds

Everyone in the play has a bond with another character, or an obligation. Some of these are fulfilled; some of these are broken.

Work with a partner

1 What obligations/bonds do these characters have?

- **a** The Duke
- **b** Shylock
- **c** Bassanio
- **d** Launcelot Gobbo
- **e** Nerissa

2 For each character, answer these questions:

- **a** Do they get an advantage from these bonds and obligations?
- **b** Are there any disadvantages for them?
- **c** Can you find scenes in which these advantages and disadvantages become clear?

Mapping bonds

Each of the main characters in *The Merchant of Venice* experiences different bonds and obligations. We can plot these on a bond map like the one at the top of next page.

Work with a partner

Choose one of these characters and make their bond map: Jessica, Portia, or Antonio.

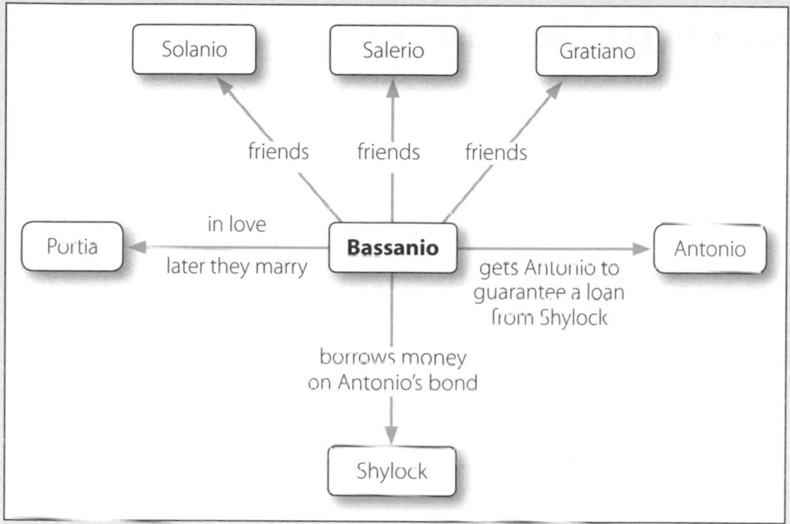

Shylock's bonds

Work with a partner

1 Make a similar bond map for Shylock.

2 Shylock suffers because other characters break their bonds with him. We can set out in a table how this happens and the results:

Character	Their bond with Shylock	How Shylock might feel when the bond is broken
Antonio	Antonio owes Shylock money/a pound of flesh.	cheated (they had a legal contract), bullied, angry, discriminated against
The Duke		
Jessica		
Launcelot Gobbo		

3 Copy and complete the table.

Work on your own

4 Imagine you are Shylock reflecting on your experiences. Write a diary entry in which you consider how you were connected to people in Venice and how you felt when obligations were broken.

Stereotypes and prejudice

Shylock claims that he is mistreated because he is Jewish: 'you called me misbeliever' (Act 1 scene 3 line 108). Equally, Shylock makes his hatred of Christians very clear, stating that he hates Antonio 'for he is a Christian' (Act 1 scene 3 line 39).

Portia's and Jessica's lives are controlled by their fathers in ways none of the male characters' lives are. Portia has to disguise herself as a man to be taken seriously in matters of law, and Jessica has to run away from home to gain her independence.

Work in a group of three or four

In the table below are five quotations from the play relating to this. Copy it out and fill in the missing information.

Quotation	Speaker	Speaking about	What it suggests about speaker's attitude
...the Jew is the very devil incarnation (Act 2 scene 2 lines 26–7)			
I am as like to call thee so again, / To spit on thee (Act 1 scene 3 lines 127–8)			
You call me misbeliever, cut-throat dog (Act 1 scene 3 line 108)			
I would she were in heaven (Act 4 scene 1 line 290)			
For this favour, he presently become a Christian (Act 4 scene 1 lines 385–6)			

'Fed with the same food': Shylock's speech

In one of the play's most famous speeches, Shylock lays his claim to be fundamentally the same as the other characters. They are united in their humanity:

> *Hath not a Jew eyes? Hath not a Jew hands, organs, dimensions, senses, affections, passions? Fed with the same food, hurt with the same weapons, subject to the same diseases, healed by the same means, warmed and cooled by the same winter and summer, as a Christian is?*
> (Act 3 scene 1 lines 54–60)

Work in a group of three or four

How well do the words and deeds of Shylock support this assertion? Find examples of similarities between Shylock and the other characters to complete this table.

Shylock	Other characters who act similarly
A merciless revenger	Portia: presses for Shylock to be killed.
A controlling father	
A ruthless merchant	
A loving husband	
A betrayed family member	

Writing task

Work on your own

Imagine you are Shylock. Write an article for the Venetian *Jewish Chronicle* arguing that Venice is a society full of prejudice.

Appearances and deception

Throughout *The Merchant of Venice* we see that things are not always what they seem, and that many characters are deceived, or do not perceive accurately. The caskets symbolise the human capacity to be misled by appearances, as it is the seemingly worthless casket which contains the prize of marriage to Portia. This theme is also evident in the trial scene, in which Portia deceives everyone except

Nerissa into thinking she is Balthasar, a learned lawyer. Antonio is equally deceived by his own fortunes. He believes at the start of the play that his ships are safe. It is under this illusion that he is willing to enter into a contract which is potentially fatal. The play provokes us to consider the implications of deceptions, and whether sometimes deceptions can be justified.

Deception in Venice

We can set out information and ideas about acts of deception in a table:

Act of deception	Who is deceived?	Why does the deception occur?	What is the effect of the deception?
Portia pretends that she wants a ring as payment.	Bassanio	Portia wants to tease Bassanio.	It creates comedy. It shows that people sometimes make promises which cannot always be kept.

Work with a partner

1 Make a similar table for these acts of deception:

  a Shylock claims that the bond of a pound of flesh is a joke.

  b Jessica dresses up as a man to run away from her father.

  c Portia dresses as Balthasar.

  d Launcelot Gobbo pretends that he has died.

2 Now find two other acts of deception in the play and add them to your table.

Who said that?

Work in a group of three or four

1 Match the speaker to the quotation.

  Speakers:

  Morocco   Portia   Shylock   Jessica   Antonio

Quotations:

- **a** *All that glisters is not gold* (Act 2 scene 7 line 65)
- **b** *But love is blind, and lovers cannot see* | *The pretty follies that themselves commit* (Act 2 scene 6 lines 36–7)
- **c** *The devil can cite Scripture for his purpose.* (Act 1 scene 3 line 95)
- **d** *They shall think we are accomplished* | *With what we lack.* (Act 3 scene 4 lines 61–2)
- **e** *How much more elder art thou than thy looks.* (Act 4 scene 1 line 250)

2 We can set out ideas about each quotation in a web diagram:

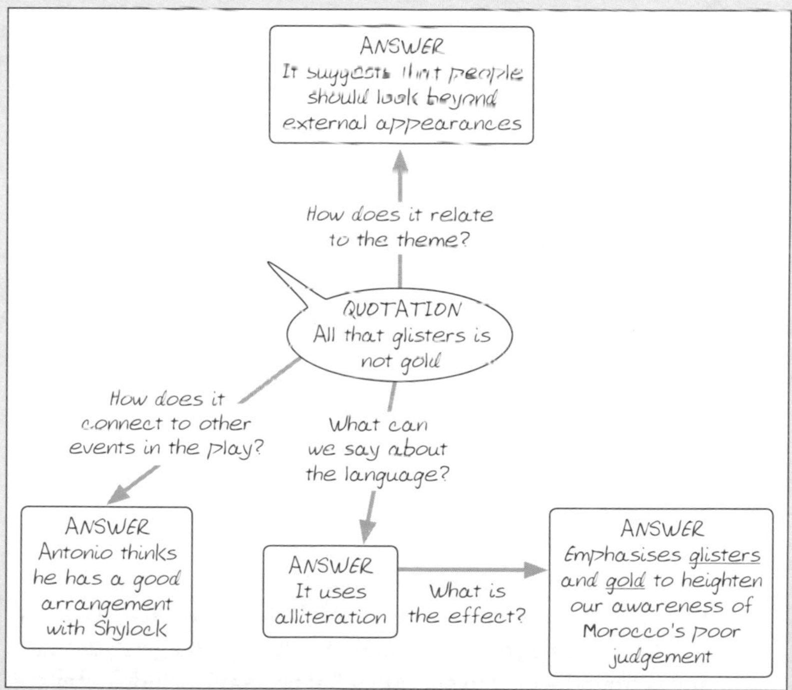

3 Create a similar diagram for the other quotations.

Presentation

Create a poster relating to the theme of 'appearances and deception'.

Justice and mercy

Justice and mercy are key themes in the Shylock and Antonio plot. Shylock seeks the strict legal justice of Antonio's punishment for a failed debt payment. In contrast, Portia claims justice is not the same as the law, and that true justice is merciful. However, Portia does not show this same mercy to Shylock when he loses his legal case. Shylock also complains that Antonio is unjust in depriving him of business by lending money interest-free; a point made more powerful by the fact that money-lending for profit was one of the few occupations open to somebody Jewish in Christian Europe. Antonio, on the other hand, believes Shylock is unjust in making money from interest on loans.

Justice in Venice

Work with a partner

1 In this play there are examples of justice and injustice in Venice. Make a list of as many as you can think of and set them out in a table like this:

Examples of injustice in Venice	Why you think these are unjust	Examples of justice in Venice	Why you think these are just

Work on your own

2 Imagine that you are either:

a a Venetian nobleman, or
b a prominent Venetian Jew.

You have been asked by the Duke to investigate how 'just' Venetian society is. Write a letter to the Duke setting out your ideas. Use the table you have made to help you and give specific examples from the play to support what you say. Include details of:

- where the law and justice match each other
- where the law and justice are in conflict

- who benefits from justice
- who suffers from injustice
- recommendations for changes.

'I stand for judgement'

There are many differing opinions on what constitutes justice in *The Merchant of Venice*. Characters' words can communicate a variety of viewpoints on justice and mercy, and can even lead us to question what we understand justice and mercy to be. Characters' opinions on justice and mercy can also convey aspects of the characters' personalities.

Work on your own

1 Here are two quotations about justice:

SHYLOCK I'll have my bond. I will not hear thee speak.
(Act 3 scene 3 line 12)

BASSANIO Wrest once the law to your authority:
To do a great right, do a little wrong...
(Act 4 scene 1 lines 214–15)

a What do each of the statements tell us about the speaker's opinion of justice and mercy?

b What does each tell us about the speaker's personality?

2 Now find three more quotations, on the same theme, from these scene sections:

- Act 1 scene 3 lines 157–67
- Act 4 scene 1 lines 182–204
- Act 4 scene 1 lines 243–60

3 Answer questions 1(a) and 1(b) about each quotation.

A pound of flesh

Work with a partner

1 Imagine you are lawyers for Shylock, and want to order a retrial. To prepare your argument, copy and complete this grid.

Portia's arguments against Shylock	Possible rebuttals
Shylock must cut out exactly one pound.	*Antonio owes the pound so it is Antonio's responsibility to remove it and provide it, not Shylock's.*
Shylock must not spill any blood.	
Shylock cannot change his mind and take back his money.	
Shylock must give up his wealth to Antonio and the state.	
Shylock must be merciful.	

The retrial

Work in a group of three

1 Each person choose one of these roles:

- Shylock's lawyer
- Portia, acting as Antonio's lawyer
- the Duke, acting as judge.

2 Rehearse a retrial in which Shylock's lawyer wants to overturn all the original decisions, and still get the flesh of Antonio.

3 Share your performance with the class.

Writing about *The Merchant of Venice*

Writing about a play is the most common form of assessment. It is also a very helpful way for you to consider and develop your ideas about the play. You can show in detail what you know and understand about the play. There are several steps you should go through to create a strong piece of writing. These are:

1 **Read:** Read the question or task carefully. Decide what is being asked of you.

2 **Think and develop:** Think about what parts of the play you will use to answer the question. Consider what points and quotations your essay will contain. Here you will also develop your comment and analysis in note form.

3 **Plan:** Plan the structure of your response.

4 **Write:** Write your response to the task or questions, using your planning notes to guide you.

5 **Edit for meaning:** Edit your first draft, making sure your writing is clear, and that your ideas make sense. Check that you have used suitable quotations, and that your analysis and comment are developed.

6 **Check for accuracy:** Check what you have written and correct any errors.

Step 1: Read

A written assessment allows you to show what you know and understand about a particular aspect of the play. The purpose of a written assessment is to check your knowledge and understanding, and for you to share your knowledge and understanding. Regardless of the question, a good answer might deal with:

- characters
- events
- language
- dramatic impact
- the relevance of the play for the time it was written
- the relevance of the play for a modern audience.

Your written response should address the question while considering these aspects.

Example

> What do any two scenes in *The Merchant of Venice* suggest about how stereotypes and prejudice affect people's lives?

The first thing to do is to identify what the question is asking you. An effective method to decide this is to underline the essential phrases, like this:

> What do <u>any two scenes</u> in *The Merchant of Venice* suggest about how <u>stereotypes and prejudice</u> <u>affect people's lives</u>?

These phrases are the key components of what you are being asked. In this case:

- the existence of stereotypes and prejudice
- the effect of these on people's lives.

Work on your own

1 Read these five tasks:

  a How does the audience's opinion of Shylock and one other character change throughout the play?

  b How is tension created in the trial scene?

  c What does *The Merchant of Venice* suggest about love and how it influences people's behaviour?

  d What does *The Merchant of Venice* suggest about the complexity of human beings?

  e What do the portrayals of Venice and of Belmont communicate about life in the two settings?

2 Copy each one, and underline what you think are the key words.

Work with a partner

3 Compare your answers with a partner. Explain why you made your choices.

Step 2: Think and develop

It is always a good idea to consider how you are going to respond to the question. This is true even in a test. Start by writing the key words from the question in a box in the centre of a blank page:

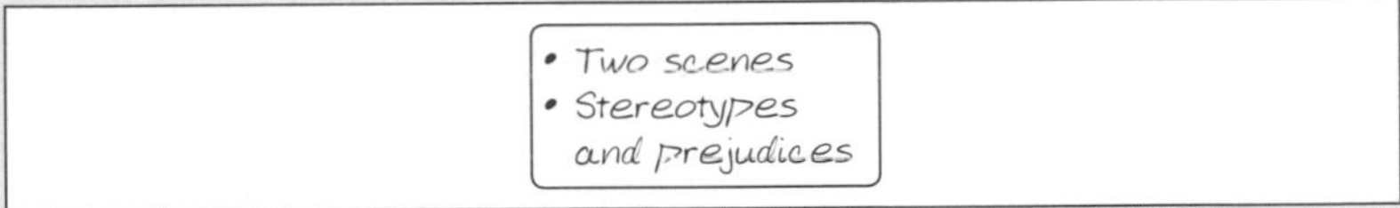

If you need to split your answer into sections, you should do that next:

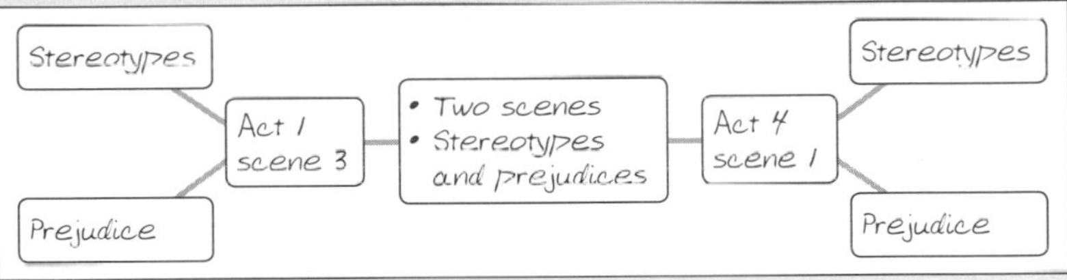

Next add some initial ideas you may wish to develop:

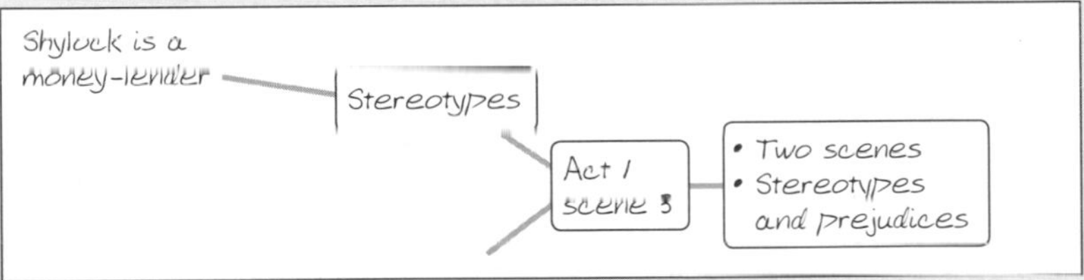

Finally, add short quotations to support your ideas, and consider how you can develop the points and quotations with further thoughts and comment. Draw lines to mark possible links between thoughts, making a 'web of ideas'. This will allow you to see connections and contrasts.

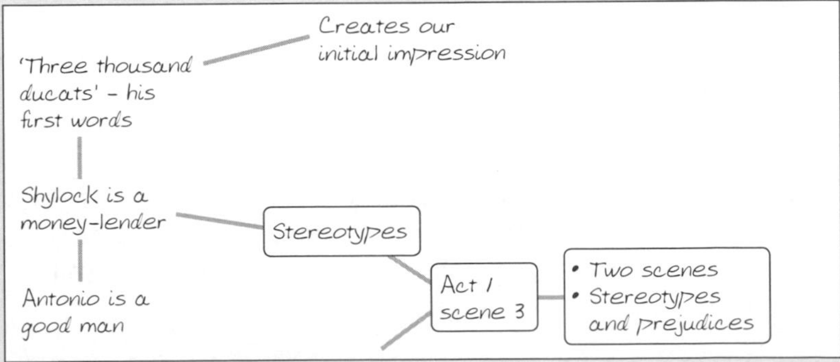

Step 3: Plan

The next stage is to make a plan. You need to give your writing a clear pattern.

Your overall pattern will be:

1 Introduction **2** Body **3** Conclusion

Introduction

Your introduction should address the question with:

- your explanation of what the question means
- why it is important.

Think about what moments of stereotyping and prejudice there are in any two scenes, and how they affect people. Address the question in your opening sentence, but don't go straight to your developed points! You should aim to give a general introduction to something you will explore in more detail in the main body. For example:

> In Act 1 scene 3, and in Act 4 scene 1, we witness several incidents of prejudicial behaviour and stereotyping, which affect different characters in different ways. Antonio comes across as a rude, racist bigot when Shylock talks of his behaviour, and our sympathy as an audience is initially given to Shylock. This is because of the cruel treatment he recounts to both Antonio and to us, the audience.

Conclusion

At the other end of your answer you should write a concluding paragraph. This should do two things:

- It should sum up the main points of your argument.
- It should set out clearly your answer to the question.

But it should *not* introduce any new evidence or ideas.

Body

Now you know how your answer begins and ends, all you have to do is plan the main part of the answer: the body! This should lead clearly from your explanation of the question (Introduction) to your explanation of the answer (Conclusion).

The body of your answer should be divided into a number of paragraphs, each of which covers an important aspect of the answer. You should look back at your web diagram to help you decide what these topics are.

What you do	Play scenes	Paragraphs
Begin with the scene you have chosen that comes earlier in the play. Write one paragraph for each of the two main characters: Antonio and Shylock, explaining how they are influenced and affected by stereotypes and prejudice.	First chosen scene	1. Shylock 2. Antonio
Now write about the main characters in your second scene, e.g. Shylock, Antonio and Portia.	Second chosen scene	3. Shylock 4. Antonio 5. Portia
The third section of your answer should look at both scenes together. Compare how the characters in the two scenes are affected by stereotypes and prejudice. Show the similarities and differences between their responses.	The two scenes	6. Similarities 7. Differences

Step 4: Write

As you write, you should try to include as many of these topics as possible:

- The characters in the play
- Its plot and structure
- The different ways in which it can be staged
- How the audience might react
- Language and imagery
- The themes and ideas explored in the play.

Remember that you have made a plan! It's easy to get away from the point as you write. Look back at your plan regularly to keep your writing on track.

Point, Evidence, and Explanation

It is no use just making statements about the play unless you can back them up. Each part of your argument should contain three elements:

1 **Point:** You express the idea you want to express.

2 **Evidence:** You refer to the text of the play, using:
   - a direct quotation, or
   - a description of something that happens in the play.

3 **Explanation:** You explain and explore how the evidence you have quoted backs up the point you are making.

Here is an example.

When we first see Antonio and Shylock together, we are told of Antonio's previous unpleasant behaviour towards Shylock [POINT]. Shylock reminds Antonio that Antonio has called him a 'misbeliever', a 'cut-throat dog' and that he has 'spit' on Shylock's 'Jewish gabardine' [EVIDENCE]. This could indicate that Antonio is someone with anti-Semitic attitudes, as two of his insults to Shylock are specifically about Shylock's Jewishness. Perhaps this would encourage the audience to feel sympathetic towards Shylock; especially as, in a Christian society like Venice, Shylock would have very little power to stop these verbal and physical attacks. However, *the audience might wonder if Shylock has done anything to draw Antonio's dislike, especially as the insult 'cut-throat dog' is not about Shylock's Jewishness, but might be about his business practices. An audience in Shakespeare's time may have considered the lending of money for interest to be against Christian charity, and so feel supportive of Antonio's behaviour* [EXPLANATION].

You may have noticed that this example uses words like 'could', 'would', 'might', and 'perhaps'. We use words like these when we want to open up ideas and not be too definite – there is always more than one possible answer to a question.

Step 5: Edit for meaning

It is tempting to think that when you have completed your first draft, your job is finished, but that would be a mistake. You now need to read through your answer to make sure it says what you wanted it to say. Imagine that you are someone else reading it, such as your teacher, or an examiner. What sense will they make of what you have written?

Ask yourself these questions:

1 Is my writing clear?
2 Does it express *exactly* what I mean?
3 Have I missed out anything important?
4 Have I used Point, Evidence, and Explanation correctly?
5 Do my sentences make sense to the reader? (Or are they confused, too long, and difficult to follow?)

Step 6: Check for accuracy

And finally, check through your writing for accuracy. Correct any mistakes you find in:

- grammar
- punctuation
- spelling.

Writing tasks and questions

Shorter tasks

1 Pick one of these scenes. Explain how drama/tension is created in the scene.

- Act 1 scene 3
- Act 3 scene 2
- Act 4 scene 1

2 Pick one of these scenes. Describe two different ways it might be performed. How would the different performances alter the audience's understanding of the scene?

- Act 3 scene 1
- Act 2 scene 9
- Act 5 scene 1

3 Pick a line spoken by any character in the play. Explain:

a what it communicates about the character

b how it relates to any of the themes

c how language is used in the line.

4 Read Act 1 scene 1 again. How do events in this scene set up events for the rest of the play?

5 Read Act 2 scene 3 and Act 2 scene 5. What do we learn about life in Shylock's house?

Creative tasks

1 Pick one of these characters: Antonio, Shylock, Bassanio, or Portia.

Write a diary entry for:

a the day before the trial of Antonio

b the evening after the trial scene.

2 Imagine you are Jessica. Write the letter she sends to Lorenzo (in Act 2 scene 3).

3 Many people in the twenty-first century write internet blogs, in which they describe events from their lives, and offer their opinions on a variety of subjects. Write a blog entry for:

a Shylock after Act 1 scene 3

b Portia after Act 2 scene 9

c Antonio after Act 5 scene 1

Longer tasks

1 Pick any two of these characters: Shylock, Antonio, Bassanio, and Portia. Explain how their relationship changes in the play.

2 Explain how the themes of 'justice and mercy' are presented in the play.

3 What does the play show us about both the benefits and the restrictions of 'bonds and obligations' in *The Merchant of Venice*?

4 Explain how language is used to explore the theme of 'stereotypes and prejudice' in the play.

5 Consider how the themes of 'love and hate' are developed in *The Merchant of Venice*.

6 Pick any character. Explain how the audience's opinion of the character might change throughout the play.

7 Is Shylock more of a wronged victim than a cold-hearted monster?

8 To what extent can it be argued that Antonio has no cause to complain that Shylock wants to kill him?

9 Imagine you are Jessica at the end of the play. Write a letter to Shylock explaining:

  a how you felt about living with him

  b what you think about him

  c why you did what you did

  d how you feel about him now.

10 Imagine you are Shylock at the end of the play. Write a letter to Jessica explaining:

  a why you treated her the way you did

  b how you felt when she left

  c why you wanted to kill Antonio

  d how you feel now.

11 Imagine you write for *The Venice Christian Times*. Write a news story about Antonio's trial.

12 Imagine you write for *The Venice Jewish Chronicle*. Write a news story about Antonio's trial.

Glossary

In these explanations, words that are in **bold** type are explained separately in this Glossary.

alliteration a figure of speech in which words close to each other begin with the same consonant sound: 'a breed of barren metal of his friend? | But lend it rather to thine enemy, | Who if he break, thou mayst with better face | Exact the penalty.' (Act 1 scene 3 lines 131–4) The repeated 'b' sound helps to draw attention to these words.

apostrophe a figure of speech in which a character speaks directly to a person who is not present or to a **personification**. For example, Shylock exclaims, 'O father Abram, what these Christians are...' (Act 1 scene 3 line 157).

aside a speech made by one of the characters for the ears of the audience alone, or purely for the benefit of another character on stage. For example, in Act 1 scene 3 when Antonio enters, Shylock has the aside, 'How like a fawning publican he looks' (line 38). See also **soliloquy**.

blank verse Shakespeare wrote his plays using a mixture of prose and verse. The lines of verse sometimes **rhymed** but more often did not rhyme. Verse that does not rhyme is called blank verse.

caesura a pause or interruption in the middle of a line of verse (from the Latin word meaning 'to cut'). For example: 'If you do love me, you will find me out' (Act 3 scene 2 line 41).

contraction shortening a word or words by missing out some of the letters. The missing letters are shown by an apostrophe. Modern examples are *she's* (for *she is*) and *shan't* (for *shall not*). In Shakespeare's time other contractions were also used, such as *'tis* (for *it is*) and *show'st* (for *showest*).

dramatic irony a situation in a play when the audience (and possibly some of the characters) know something one or more of the characters do not. In a pantomime, for example, young children will often shout to tell the hero that a dreadful monster is creeping up behind him, unseen. For example: in Act 4 scene 1 Bassanio tells Antonio he would be prepared to sacrifice everything, even his wife to save his life (lines 281 6). We know, but he doesn't, that his wife is actually standing right next to him.

end-on staging a form of staging in which the audience sit in rows all facing the same way with the stage at one end.

enjambement sometimes in blank verse there is a natural pause at the end of a line. At other times there is no break and the sentence just runs over onto the next line. For example: 'He lends out money gratis, and brings down | The rate of usance here with us in Venice' (Act 1 scene 3 lines 41–2). This running on is called enjambement (from the French word for 'span').

exeunt a Latin word meaning 'They go away', used for the departure of characters from a scene.

exit a Latin word meaning 'He (or she) goes away', used for the departure of a character from a scene.

extended image most **images** are fairly short, taking up no more than a line or two. Sometimes a writer builds up an image so that it runs on for several lines. This is called an extended image. For example: 'The scarfed bark puts from her native bay, | Hugged and embraced by the strumpet wind. | How like the prodigal doth she return, | With over-weathered ribs and ragged sails, | Lean, rent, and beggared by the strumpet wind' (Act 2 scene 6 lines 15–19).
When a ship first sails it is in good condition and the weather is favourable. By the time it returns it is in poor condition. This image is used to illustrate how love starts passionately but grows weaker as time passes.

figurative language language used that is not literally true, usually for some kind of special effect. **Metaphors** and **similes** are examples of figurative language. For example, the beginning of Portia's famous speech: 'The quality of mercy is not strained, | It droppeth as the gentle rain from heaven' (Act 4 scene 1 lines 183–4).

hyperbole deliberate exaggeration, for dramatic effect. For example, when Bassanio opens the casket and sees Portia's portrait he exclaims, 'What demi-god | Hath come so near creation?' (Act 3 scene 2 lines 115–16)

iambic pentameter a line of **verse** which contains ten syllables, with a repeated pattern of weak and strong beats:
*Thou **art** too **wild**, too **rude** and **bold** of **voice***
(ti **tum** ti **tum** ti **tum** ti **tum** ti **tum**)
See also **metre, rhythm**.

imagery — **figurative language** in which the writer communicates an idea by creating a picture in the mind of the reader or listener. Types of figurative language include **metaphors** and **similes**.

irony — when someone says one thing and means another. Sometimes it is used to tease or satirise someone, or it can express great bitterness. For example, in Act 1 scene 2 Portia says of one of her suitors, 'why he hath a horse better than the Neapolitan's, a better bad habit of frowning than the Count Palatine; he is every man in no man' (lines 58–60). She doesn't mean this literally of course; she is reporting his own view of himself and as she admits 'mocking' him. See also **dramatic irony**.

metaphor — a figure of speech in which one person, or thing, or idea is described as if it were another. For example, Portia comments on the Prince of Arragon's distress at his failure to choose the right casket: 'Thus hath the candle singed the moth' (Act 2 scene 9 line 78). The challenge of the caskets is both attractive and dangerous, as a candle is to a moth, and the Prince is foolish (as moths appear to be) and gets hurt.

metre — the regular pattern of weak and strong beats in a line of verse. The most common metre in Shakespeare's plays is iambic. Each section consists of two syllables. The first is weak and the second is strong. See **iambic pentameter**.

myth — a traditional story, usually very old. Myths often explain important events in the life of a people and they sometimes refer to the lives of gods or other supernatural creatures.

onomatopoeia using words that are chosen because they mimic the sound of what is being described.

oxymoron **figurative language** in which the writer combines two ideas which are opposites. This frequently has a startling or unusual effect. For example, in Act 2 scene 6 Jessica declares, 'lovers cannot see | The pretty follies that themselves commit' (lines 36–7).

personification referring to a thing or an idea as if it were a person. For example, in Act 5 scene 1 Lorenzo sees the stars as angels: 'There's not the smallest orb which thou behold'st | But in his motion like an angel sings...' (lines 60–1).

play on words see **pun**.

prose the form of language that is used for normal written communication. It is contrasted with **verse**.

proverb a common saying that is used by many people. Proverbs usually express something that is useful knowledge, or that people think is useful. For example, 'Many hands make light work'. Shakespeare often uses proverbs in his plays. For example, in Act 2 scene 7 the verse written on the scroll inside the golden casket begins with the words, 'All that glisters is not gold...' (line 65).

pun a figure of speech in which the writer uses a word that has more than one meaning. Both meanings of the word are used to make a joke. An example is when Gratiano says of Jessica, 'Now, by my hood, a gentle and no Jew' (Act 2 scene 6 line 51). There is a pun in 'gentle' meaning friendly, kind and softly-mannered and 'gentile' – someone who is not Jewish.

rhetorical question a question used for effect, usually in argument or debate, sometimes in a **soliloquy**. An answer is not expected. It would break the flow of the speech if it were offered. For example, Shylock says of himself and his fellow Jews, 'If you prick us do we not bleed?' (Act 3 scene 1 lines 60–1).

rhyme when two lines of **verse** end with the same sound, they are said to rhyme. Shakespeare often makes use of rhyme, both in the middle of scenes and to round them off. For example: 'I am glad on't, I desire no more delight | Than to be under sail, and gone tonight' (Act 2 scene 6 lines 67–8).

rhythm the pattern of weak and strong syllables in a piece of writing. Shakespeare writes in **iambic pentameters**, but varies the way he uses them by breaking the rules. So his lines are mainly regular but with a lot of small variations. This combination makes up the rhythm of the verse. For example, the rhythm of Portia's speech at the beginning of Act 3 scene 2 (lines 1–24) follows the pattern of her thoughts. She doesn't want Bassanio to choose just yet in case he chooses wrongly, and she doesn't want to admit that she loves him. The jerky rhythm of the lines reflects her inner agitation.

satire making fun of something that you dislike or wish to criticise, by sending it up in some way.

simile a comparison between two things which the writer makes clear by using words such as 'like' or 'as'. For example, Bassanio says of Portia, 'her sunny locks | Hang on her temples like a golden fleece...' (Act 1 scene 1 lines 169–70).

soliloquy when a character is alone on stage, or separated from the other characters in some way and speaks either apparently to himself or herself, or directly to the audience. For example: Launcelot Gobbo has a soliloquy in Act 2 scene 2 lines 1–30, when he deliberates about leaving Shylock's service.

theatre-in-the-round a form of theatre in which the audience sit on all sides of the acting area.

thrust stage a form of theatre in which the stage projects out into the audience, who thus sit on three sides of it. Shakespeare's Globe Theatre was like this, and so is the modern one in London, and the new Royal Shakespeare Theatre in Stratford-upon-Avon.

verse writing that uses regular patterns, such as **metre** and **rhyme**.